I0882899

Advance Praise

"However hard I try to devise engaging writing topics, my ideas routinely fall flat. Why? Because they are mine. Katherine Schulten suggests a more effective approach—asking students to write about issues they care about—for example, why we should all eat more bugs. If you are suffering from the five-paragraph essay blues, these student essays offer fledgling writers models of what's possible in persuasive writing. They demonstrate how risk-taking pays off."

—Carol Jago, high school English teacher, past president of the National Council of Teachers of English, and author of *The Book in Question: Why and How Reading is in Crisis* (Heinemann, 2019)

"It is no secret that The New York Times Learning Network, and Katherine Schulten in particular, have long been a friend of the classroom teacher. This newest offering is no exception—providing everything a teacher needs for robust, authentic instruction in argumentative writing. The powerful essays provide vision and inspiration for student writers, while the instructional guide gives teachers step-by-step guidance for amplifying student voice and taking student writing to new heights. Simply put, this work is a gift."

—Rebekah O'Dell, author of *Beyond Literary Analysis* and *Writing With Mentors*, and cofounder of MovingWriters.org

"The essays in *Student Voice* loudly proclaim what young writers are capable of: insightful opinions, thoughtful argument, compelling evidence, and—most importantly—lively writing. They will inspire young writers everywhere. And for teachers who hope for writing like this in their own classrooms, *Raising Student Voice* provides them with a teaching companion to help them along."

—Elyse Eidman-Aadahl, Executive Director, National Writing Project

"I think it's safe to say that many—if not most—of us teachers are always trying to figure out better ways to assist our students in becoming better writers. Katherine Schulten's two books are the best resources that have come along in years to help us do just that! They're filled with exceptional instructional strategies and marvelous examples and mentor texts. What's not to love?"

—Larry Ferlazzo, high school teacher, author, and Ed Week teacher advice columnist

"I love this book. It practices what it preaches by being crisp, well written, and to-the-point. I want a copy now to hand out to my whole department."

—Alexis Wiggins, author of *The Best Class You Never Taught* and English Department Chair at The John Cooper School in The Woodlands, TX

"Mentor texts from students are essential, and yet it is really hard to find good ones. The essays in *Student Voice* are marvelous, especially in regard to their voices, accessibility, range, and diversity. And the 35 points made in the teacher's companion, *Raising Student Voice*, are wonderful; I love the voices of teachers, students, and argumentation experts."

—Matthew Johnson, author of *Flash Feedback: Responding to Student Writing Better and Faster—Without Burning Out*

RAISING STUDENT VOICE

Norton Books in Education

RAISING STUDENT VOICE

35 Ways to Help Students Write Better Argument Essays, from *The New York Times*

A Teacher's Companion to *Student Voice: 100 Argument Essays by Teens on Issues That Matter to Them*

KATHERINE SCHULTEN

W. W. NORTON & COMPANY
Independent Publishers Since 1923

Note to Readers: Models and/or techniques described in this volume are illustrative or are included for general informational purposes only; neither the publisher nor the author(s) can guarantee the efficacy or appropriateness of any particular recommendation in every circumstance.

Printed in the United States of America
First Edition

Manufacturing by LSC Harrisonburg
Book design by Vicki Fischman
Production manager: Katelyn MacKenzie

ISBN: 978-0-393-71432-6 (pbk.)

W. W. Norton & Company, Inc., 500 Fifth Avenue, New York, N.Y. 10110
www.wwnorton.com

W. W. Norton & Company Ltd., 15 Carlisle Street, London W1D 3BS

2 3 4 5 6 7 8 9 0

Contents

Acknowledgments

In the acknowledgments to *Student Voice*, I thanked the many people at The New York Times and W. W. Norton who contributed to these books, but here I'd like to focus on the teachers and students who gave their time and ideas to make this Companion possible.

First, to the teenagers who agreed to be interviewed and share their writing process: talking to you was my very favorite part of doing this work. Thank you to Anushka Agarwal, Angela Chen, Narain Dubey, Nora Fellas, Lila McNamee, Asaka Park, Bridget Smith, Noah Spencer, and Tony Xiao—and please, all of you, keep writing.

Next, to the many talented teachers who generously shared their thinking: I never yearned to be back in a classroom more than when I was listening to each of you describe yours. Thank you to Donna Amit-Cubbage, Erica Lee Beaton, Seth Czarnecki, Christa Forster, Sarah Gross, Shari Krapels, Amanda Lentino, Beth Pandolpho, Amy Robinson, Susan Rothbard, and Alissa Warren—and to Jacqueline Hesse and Christine McCartney for their ideas and for the lovely day I spent with them and their students at Newburgh Free Academy P-TECH. Finally, a special thanks to Kabby Hong, whose deep belief in encouraging student voice became the backbone of this guide.

An invisible team of teacher-readers helped make the book you hold in your hands much better than it was in its first draft. Thank you for your advice and observations, Bob Fecho, Matthew Johnson, Jonna Kuskey, and Gerri Woods.

But nothing I write about teaching and learning is ever complete until I acknowledge the debt I owe The New York City Writing Project, my local site of the mighty National Writing Project. Their 1987 Summer Invitational seminar at Lehman College in The Bronx introduced me, at 24, to everything important I still know and believe about teaching and learning, and the wider Writing Project community has been my best source of inspiration ever since.

Introduction

The essays in this collection have been chosen from over 43,000 submitted by teenagers around the world to the annual New York Times Learning Network Student Editorial Contest.

Some are heartbreaking and some are funny. Some take on problems of global importance like climate change and immigration, while others focus on smaller issues that nonetheless loom large in the lives of teenagers, from selfie culture to bullying in gym class.

Some writers use personal experiences to make arguments, while others build them chiefly through facts and logic. One boy who traveled across America in his family's minivan shares details from his adventures to advocate for the "wonders of wandering," while the writer of "The Integrity of Pineapple Pizza" makes a science-based case for the tastiness and nutritional value of a food that has, according to her, "been disrespected for far too long."

If your students think persuasive writing is a dull, paint-by-numbers genre useful mainly for standardized tests, I hope these 100 essays can convince them otherwise. If they see argumentation as strictly a school-based skill, I hope the pieces can show them how it works in a real-world context, for an audience beyond the teacher.

And if your students believe that the word "I" has no place in formal writing, I'm confident this collection can prove to them just how powerful personal stories can be. From an essay by a Lipan Apache boy questioning Native American stereotypes, to a piece by a disabled girl called "Social Media is My Lifeline," the writing in these pages is richer for the ways students have grounded it in lived experience.

As the educator and author Grant Wiggins has noted, "The point of writing is to have something to say and to make a difference in saying it. Rarely, however, is *impact* the focus of writing instruction in English class."[1]

Impact is very much the focus of our contest and the rationale behind publishing this book. Every spring since 2014, we've invited students to choose any issue they like, and, in no more than 450 words, convince us that we should care. Our judges—writers and editors from the *Times* Opinion section and The Learning Network, as well as educators from around the country—pick the pieces that do that best. The winners are then published on our site, and, often, excerpted in print in *The New York Times*.

The goal of this Teacher's Companion is to help you use these essays as mentor texts for your own students. To show them "writer's moves" made not by professionals, but by kids their own age—and, more importantly, to convince them that they, too, have something to say.

At a time when examples of "student voice" are everywhere, from Malala Yousafzai to Greta Thunberg to the Parkland students, the argument writing that students study in school is still almost entirely written by adults—"by, like, 50-year-old white guys who have been doing this for their whole careers," as one student I interviewed put it.

It is a wholly different experience for teenagers to study the work of fellow 13 to 18-year-olds. It's relatable. It's relevant. And it doesn't feel like an untouchable ideal, something you could achieve yourself only after you acquired multiple degrees.

In other words, none of the essays in this collection are perfect, and no one would expect them to be. In fact, that is one of their virtues: students can have conversations with them. As Jaden Caballero, a junior at Newburgh Free Academy P-TECH in Newburgh, New York, said as his class discussed one of the pieces, "This kid has moves, but I have moves, too. I could learn something from her, but she could learn something from me, too."

Jaden's teachers, Jacqueline Hesse and Christine McCartney, let me bring a few of the winning 2019 essays to show their students, all of whom are well-practiced in analyzing and employing rhetorical strategies themselves. That class's reaction—that the work was approachable and interesting in terms of topic, tone, language, and message, and that it could inspire their own writing—echoes what we hear from those who work with our contest every year.

For instance, Kabby Hong, an English teacher in Verona, Wisconsin, whose students are often finalists, and whose advice is woven throughout this guide, says he first came upon the contest just as he was tiring of the "lifeless" essays his class was producing.

"You can tell when they don't care," he says. "Not only were those papers not enjoyable for my students to write, I wasn't having fun reading them either."

What Mr. Hong likes most about our challenge is that "kids don't choose the topics adults think they should choose."

"When we read the work of the winners, I see my students nodding their heads, like, 'I feel that way too.' At first they're tentative about their own writing, but after they see winning essays on things they never thought you could write about in school—gender identity, academic pressure, social media—they relax. You can see they feel like there's a big broad field they can play in," he says.

So consider this collection an argument, too. An argument that if we believe student voice is truly meaningful, then helping kids figure out what they want to say and how they want to say it should be a significant focus of the time they spend in school. An argument that students write better when they have some choice over the topic and form, when they write for an audience beyond the teacher and a purpose beyond a grade, and when they get to sound like themselves.

In the student anthology you'll find 100 different examples of just that, and to help your classes do the same, whether for our contest or any other purpose, this Teacher's Companion offers detailed advice for every stage of the process, most of it drawn from the winners themselves. The annotated essay index that follows will give you a taste of the themes and individual topics your students will be able to read about in the *Student Voice* anthology.

Index to the 100 Essays in the *Student Voice* Anthology

TEENAGE LIFE ONLINE

TEENAGE LIFE OFFLINE

SCHOOL

CIVIC LIFE AND POLITICS

GENDER AND SEXUALITY

SCIENCE, TECHNOLOGY, AND THE ENVIRONMENT

PHYSICAL AND MENTAL HEALTH

ARTS, CULTURE, AND FOOD

More About The Essays and The New York Times Learning Network

All the essays in **Student Voice: 100 Argument Essays by Teens on Issues That Matter to Them** were either winners or runners-up in one of our Student Editorial Contests between 2014 and 2019 and were chosen for this book from among many because they represent a range of evergreen issues. If your students would like to participate, we run the contest annually in February, and rules and details—as well as lesson plans and other resources—are on our site.[2] Nowhere online, however, can you find this full collection, nor the material in this Teacher's Companion.

To write the Teacher's Companion, I interviewed as many of the student winners and their teachers as I could. Though like everyone on staff at The Learning Network I am a former teacher, these days I sit in a newsroom instead of a classroom, and I wanted most of the ideas to come from current practitioners.

In case you're not familiar with our site, it has been part of NYTimes.com since 1998 and has had the same mission for over 20 years—to help people teach and learn with *Times* content and thereby "bring the world into the classroom."

Over time, however, our focus has changed significantly. In 1998 nytimes.com/learning was chiefly a place for teachers to get lesson plans. Today it is better known as a hub for student commentary on everything from politics to pop culture. We hear from nearly 1,500 teenagers a week as they post thoughts to our daily writing prompts and to our weekly discussions about *Times* photos, films, and graphics. We also run ten annual contests that invite students to write editorials as well as create videos, political cartoons, poems, reviews, photo essays, podcasts, and more. We'd be delighted to have your students join us, too.

How To Use This Book

Whether you are just introducing argument writing to a middle school class or working with AP students who are experts on rhetoric, the 100 essays in the *Student Voice* anthology can help.

- They can serve as approachable, peer-to-peer mentor texts for the kinds of sophisticated "moves" your students might make in their own writing.
- They can show how varied the voices, topics, tones, and styles of real-world opinion writing can be and prove that it doesn't have to follow an unyielding set of rules.
- They can be paired with adult writing on similar themes or issues to offer additional perspectives and show young people that their voices can contribute to a larger conversation.
- But above all, the 100 selected essays and these materials that accompany them can, I hope, inspire your students to do their *own* writing on the issues that matter the most to them.

Here is how the materials in the anthology and teacher's companion guide are organized.

THE TEACHER'S COMPANION

Raising Student Voice: 35 Ways to Help Students Write Better Argument Essays, from The New York Times

- Introduction
- An Index to the Essays in the Anthology

- Instructional Strategies: Five sections of practical advice gathered from the *Times* Opinion section and The Learning Network, as well as via interviews with some of the winning students, and over a dozen teachers who use our contest in their classrooms.

  Each point in the process is explained with examples from the student essays and is accompanied by a "Try this" activity you can do with your own students.

  - Reading Like Writers: Using These Essays as Mentor Texts
  - Finding a Topic: Helping Your Students Identify and Hone Their Own Arguments
  - Getting Beyond the Echo Chamber: Researching for a Range of Viewpoints
  - Composing and Revising: Tackling the Elements of an Argument Essay
  - Finding Authentic Audiences: Getting Student Work Out Into the World

- Writing Prompts: 500 prompts for argumentative writing, drawn from a decade of daily questions posted on The New York Times Learning Network. Each question was originally inspired by a piece published in the *Times*.
- Additional materials that you can use to help students find and hone their own arguments, craft their essays, and learn more about how writing is evaluated. The first two are also included in the essay anthology.

  - Appendix A: A "Topic Generator" with 16 questions to help students brainstorm writing ideas
  - Appendix B: A "before" and "after": the first and final draft of one student's winning essay
  - Appendix C: A sample essay annotated with the comments of our judges
  - Appendix D: The rubric and rules for our annual Student Editorial Contest

- Appendix E: "Essays for Teaching Various Elements of Argument": a quick-reference chart listing essays that provide clear examples of the effective use of elements like ethos, logos, and pathos

THE ESSAY ANTHOLOGY
Student Voice: 100 Argument Essays by Teens on Issues That Matter to Them

- Introduction
- 100 award-winning essays, organized into 12 categories:
  - Teenage Life Online
  - Teenage Life Offline
  - School
  - Civic Life and Politics
  - Gender and Sexuality
  - Race and Religion
  - Science, Technology, and the Environment
  - Physical and Mental Health
  - Arts, Culture, and Food
  - Sports and Gaming
  - Criminal Justice and Policing
  - Consumer Culture
- Appendix A: The Rubrics and Rules for the NYTLN Student Editorial Contest
- Appendix B: Covid-19 and the Teen Response: Three Essays from Our Spring 2020 Contest

RAISING STUDENT VOICE

Instructional Strategies: 35 Tips for Teaching with the Student Essays

INTRODUCING THESE ESSAYS TO YOUR STUDENTS

If the argumentative essays your students are most experienced with are the kinds that follow a set formula, they need to know something right away: these are not those.

Instead, the models students emulate for our contest are the short, compelling opinion pieces you can find on the Op-Ed pages of the *Times* or any other newspaper, where the goal, first and foremost, is to engage the reader—with voice, with story, and with rhetorical flourishes, as well as with reliable evidence.

To show your students the difference you might start with this scenario:

Imagine you open your local newspaper to the Opinion section and see two pieces. One is headlined "The Problem of Sexism in the Media" while the other is called "Why I, a Heterosexual Teenage Boy, Want to See More Men in Speedos."

Which are you likely to read first? Why?

Now let's compare first paragraphs. Here's how "The Problem of Sexism in the Media" begins:

> *According to women-s.net, gender stereotypes still remain one of the main problems of modern societies. They influence everything from the advertising we see to the news we read, and shape the opportunities women are offered at every stage of their lives. We must fight stereotypes that block progress to gender equality.*

Here's how "Why I . . ." starts:

> *The Sports Illustrated Swimsuit edition recently celebrated its 50th birthday. As an 18-year-old heterosexual male, I was happy to join in the festivities. However, one section of the magazine left me feeling something less than festive.*

Which makes you want to keep reading? Why?

These two essays concern the same general topic, but the first one is pretty standard—a safe recitation of arguments your students have likely read many times before. The second is surprising. It starts with an interesting personal hook, and makes us curious: What section of Sports Illustrated left this writer feeling "less than festive"? Why?

While the first essay might pass a standardized test, it reads like that is its only purpose. The second, on the other hand, is so memorable that students have been copying the headline ever since it won our first-ever Student Editorial Contest back in 2014. So effective is it at setting up a counterintuitive argument that every year we get a handful of essays entitled "Why I, a ______, Want ______." (Some of them even go on to be finalists, including **#85**, "Why I, a High School Football Player, Want to See Tackle Football Taken Away.")

To be clear, I wrote "Sexism in the Media" myself, trying to imitate the many we receive every year that don't get beyond Round 1. They're fine on the surface. There may be little technically wrong with them (though if you're going to lead with a source, a more recognized authority than women-s.net might be better), but there's also nothing memorable, nothing that makes you want to keep reading. And while making your teacher want to keep reading is probably low on your list of priorities if you're writing solely for a grade, it is the first thing you have to think about if you are trying to communicate with a real audience.

To see the contrast, have students turn to **#47** and read Noah Spencer's full "Why I" piece. Noah is now an economist working for the Canadian government, but at the time he wrote it he was a 17-year-old boy who read a lot in his free time and loved Kurt Vonnegut and Bill Bryson. Through them, he says now, "I was realizing you could put a lot of voice in your writing and produce something effective."

Many of these pieces play it stylistically safer than Noah's, yet all still find ways to hook their audience. Your students might read **#91** to see how Erica Kirchhof shows us why doping in horse-racing is a serious issue, or **#88** to note how Julianne Yu frames her argument that school systems that spend too much on athletics are a threat to democracy. Both are more traditional, but both pull you in and make you think. You can feel that these writers care about what they are saying.

One of the chief goals of the writing contests we run on The Learning Network each year is to show students how the genres and formats they learn in school translate to the real world, then invite them to make that leap in their own work.

Our narrative writing challenge, for example, uses the many different kinds of personal essays the *Times* publishes to show students how small, true stories about individual lives can make universal points—then invites them to craft their own. Our review-writing contest focuses on the similarities between that classroom classic, the literature essay, and the critical book, movie, theater, TV, and music reviews that appear in the paper, showing how both require close reading of a work in order to analyze it, explore its context, and make an argument about its worth.

To prepare students to enter each contest, we try to demystify what professional writers do. For our annual Student Editorial Contest, then, we suggest exercises like having students "adopt a columnist" to become familiar with the writer's voice, issues, and rhetorical strategies.

This book takes teenage writers just as seriously. The premise of the collection is that your students can learn just as many and varied "craft moves" from these essays as they can from the work of professional writers, and that learning from kids their own age might just be both enjoyable and empowering.

So let your classes identify the things other students have done that they admire—but also, perhaps, find places where the work could be stronger. Let them listen to the way different voices emerge in the essays, even though they're only 450 words each. Let them see how these teenagers weave in evidence of many kinds, how they vary fact and opinion, and how they support claims from "It's time to legalize prostitution" to "We should all eat more bugs." But most of all, let them read for inspiration, to figure out what *they* want to say.

Now, let's get practical. Here are 35 ways to do it.

I. Reading Like Writers: Using These Essays As Mentor Texts

Whether you have a class set of the anthology and your students are choosing their own essays, or whether everyone in the room is working with the same piece, you might begin by asking your students to think about two questions as they read:

- What do you notice or admire about this essay?
- What lessons might it have for your own writing?

Starting this way immediately positions these pieces as mentor texts with craft lessons to impart. It also puts your students in charge of surfacing what they think is most successful or interesting about each.

Below, a few more structures that can help guide close reading. Like all the advice in this book, any of this can, of course, be followed in any order, and mixed and tweaked to fit your class and curriculum.

➤ Observe How These Student Writers "Break the Rules"

If your class is new to the kind of opinion writing featured in this collection, you might need to point out to them how these essays break what they might think of as "the rules."

For instance, they may assume that all argumentative essays need to be five (or six) paragraphs long, with a thesis statement at the end of the first paragraph; that topic sentences must sit at the top of every body paragraph; and that a neat "in conclusion" should end the essay with a restatement of the thesis.

They may assume that one should never use the word "I," and that, if they're sending their work to our contest, they should take out a thesaurus and replace their everyday words with bigger ones since, after all, they're writing for *The New York Times*.

Instead, they'll find almost nothing in this collection that follows that five-paragraph formula, but they *will* come across one-sentence paragraphs everywhere they look. They'll find the frequent use of "I," sometimes to tell highly sensitive personal stories. They'll find sentence fragments galore, along with teen slang and social media–speak, and they'll also come across sarcasm and dark humor about topics they may have believed could only be discussed earnestly.

The key, of course, is helping them see when, how, and why these essays play with structure, language, and tone to get their larger points across. The next "try this" exercise, "Go behind the scenes of our judging," might help with that.

Seth Czarnecki, an English teacher in Massachusetts, says he uses our contest to free his classes up from perceptions about writing that have stifled them in the past.

"As I've started to figure out who I am as a teacher and what I value, I've realized that my students' writing was suffering because they felt they had no stake in it beyond the grade," he says. "There was that ancient pattern—read a book, write an essay, read a book, write an essay—and the joy of both reading and writing was getting lost. I wanted them to make their voices prominent, research things they cared about, use the first person, do everything you're told not to do in a formal literary analysis."

Of course, everyone on our staff is a former teacher, and we all want students to be able to write excellent formal literary analyses of classic books. We're just suggesting that students might experiment to see how some of those skills can translate to writing for audiences and purposes outside academia.

Here's an exercise that may help.

Try This:

Choose one essay from this collection and ask students to note all the "rules" they think it breaks. For instance, they might choose "Nothing

Comes Between Me and My Sushi . . . Except Plastic, Maybe" (**#62**), the piece I deal with more fully in the exercise that follows this one.

Then, invite students to compare this essay with what a more formal, academic piece on the same topic might look and sound like. You might pose questions like:

- What similarities would they have? How might they be different? How would this essay need to be rewritten to fit the standards of an academic essay?
- What is the audience and purpose for each? How might that account for some of the differences?
- Do you think you need to learn to write both kinds of essays? Why or why not?

Then, if your students would like to see an example of a more traditional essay, one that *does* follow that six-paragraph formula for argumentative writing many students learn, yet makes just as compelling a case as any in this collection, they might turn to **#16** to read "Accountability-Based Testing is Broken."

Since they will no doubt have some opinions on and experiences with the topic of testing themselves, they might think about ways they could write about the same issue, but perhaps in the looser style of a piece like "Why I, A Teenage Boy . . ." or "Nothing Comes Between Me and My Sushi." Which feels more natural to them? Are some topics better for one style than for another, or can any topic be written about in a variety of ways depending on audience and purpose?

To find four more examples of essays in this collection that are structured in a fairly traditional way, see Appendix E.

➤ Go Behind the Scenes to Listen in on Our Judging

Judging a contest like this one that receives over 10,000 entries each year requires many rounds and many readers. We always have a panel of judges that come from within the *Times*—editors on The Learning Network as well as writers and editors from the Opinion section—and we always invite another panel of judges from outside the *Times*—usually trusted high school educators from schools that are not participating in the contest. And, of course, we judge blind: until we choose our winners, we don't know anything at all about the authors of these submissions.

As you might imagine, the final round is the hardest. At that point, we have to choose from roughly 100 wonderful essays, the top 1 percent that have made it through many previous cuts, and narrow them to 50 or so finalists. Those are then further ranked to become, roughly, our top 10 winners, 15 runners-up, and 25 honorable mentions.

Though all the earlier rounds are done individually, we do this final task live. Invite your students to put themselves in our shoes and judge one of these essays, then compare their thoughts with what we said about it ourselves.

Try This:

Have your students imagine that they've read hundreds of student essays over the previous several weeks, but that today they're meeting other judges in a conference room in *The New York Times* building in midtown Manhattan to choose the finalists. On the table are pens and highlighters in many colors, stacks of our rubric (Appendix D), and copies of the essays that have made it through six previous rounds of judging.

The first one they'll discuss: "Nothing Gets Between Me and My Sushi . . . Except Plastic, Maybe" (**#62**). Have them read the piece individually, annotating to note the various things they want to point out in the group discussion that will follow. Then, invite them to have a conversation. Is this essay a top winner? Why or why not? What specific aspects would they point to to answer that question?

When they're finished they can turn to Appendix C to see some of the comments our staff made about this piece. Does our conversation echo anything your students said? What questions, if any, do our annotations raise for them? What lessons might this exercise offer for their own writing?

➤ Do a Formal Analysis of the Elements of Argumentative Essays

None of the essays in this collection could have won our contest without powerful examples of what some teachers shorthand as "CER"—claim, evidence and reasoning.

Here are two strategies teachers have told us they use to have their students close-read this work for those elements and others.

Try These:

- **Annotate for structure.**

Have your students read with pen in hand to look closely at how one or more of these essays is built, pulling back to observe the function of each paragraph, zooming in to think about individual lines and words, and then reflecting on how they work together to make an argument and support it. Where can they find elements of any argument essay, like a central claim or thesis, the evidence to back it up, and an acknowledgement of counterclaims? Does anything about the way the writer structured the argument surprise them?

Then have them discuss their findings in small groups or as a whole class. You might ask, How well did this structure work to make and support this argument? What specific "writer's moves" did that best? What if anything in the essay *didn't* work for you? Why?

- **Or borrow a useful set of guiding questions from a New Jersey educator.**

Beth Pandolpho, a teacher in New Jersey who works with our contest annually, suggests[3] that her students read some of the winning essays and answer questions like these:

- What is the author's position and main argument?
- What relevant background information does the author provide?
- How does this help you understand the argument?
- How do outside sources help support the main argument?
- What lines in the essay are opinion? What are facts? What conclusions can you draw about the mix? How do they work together?

- Where does the author acknowledge counterclaims or an opposing viewpoint?
- What is the call to action? In other words, what should people do, think, or feel as a result of reading this piece?
- Is the title provocative? Does it arouse your curiosity? How is it effective?

➤ Show Students a "Before" and "After" Essay to See How One Student Revised

Seventeen-year-old Nora Fellas, a 2019 winner, has generously allowed us to reprint her first draft of 743 words alongside her final draft of 450. Turn to Appendix B to see both.

Try This:

After they have read the essays, your students might discuss these questions:

- What differences do you notice? This writer cut nearly 300 words from her first version. Where did she make those cuts?
- Why do you think Nora made the changes she did?
- Focus on how the two pieces end. Which is stronger? Then read in Appendix B about why Nora made that change specifically.
- What can they learn from this comparison that might apply to their own work?

➤ Focus on Just the Three Basic Rhetorical Moves

Some of the teenagers who submit essays to our annual competition are students in an AP Language and Composition class somewhere, and those students have been rigorously trained in rhetorical analysis. For them, terms like *ethos, pathos,* and *logos* are part of daily discussions—and they can likely wield *kairos, anaphora,* and *epiphora*, too.

Part of our goal in using these student essays as mentor texts is to demystify this kind of writing for everyone, and make students realize that, even if they have never heard these terms, they probably intuitively understand the concepts. With a brief explanation, they'll begin to see that these appeals are everywhere from acne-medication ads to political speeches, and realize that they, too, naturally employ them in ordinary conversation.

Later in this guide, we'll show them how to weave them into their own work, but, for now, you might borrow this simple and engaging explanation by journalist Sam Leith from his *Times* essay "Other Men's Flowers"[4]:

> *Rhetoric, simply put, is the study of how language works to persuade. So any writer seeking to make a case, or hold a reader's attention—which is more or less any writer not in the service of the Democratic People's Republic of Korea—has something to learn from it.*

Here's how Mr. Leith sums up ethos, pathos, and logos:

> *It does help to keep in mind that, as Aristotle wrote, you have three forms of power over the reader: ethos, pathos and logos. That is, roughly: selling yourself, swaying the emotions and advancing your argument. Any sentence you write should be pulling one or more of those levers; the best will do all three. Even apparent decoration works to a purpose—if a phrase is beautiful, funny or memorable, it is doing work on its audience.*

Try This:

Challenge your students to read just to find the words, phrases, and sentences in the student essays that they think are "doing work on" their audience. That is, what lines jump out at them, for any reason? Which made them feel a strong emotion? Which made them stop and think? Which made them question? Which made them put their trust in the writer?

Then, ask them to analyze how:

- Is the line citing facts and making the appeals to reason that are hallmarks of a logos appeal?
- Does it use pathos to make an emotional connection, perhaps via a story or through carefully chosen language that provokes anger or empathy?

- Does it describe a personal experience or connection that speaks to the author's own authority, or ethos, on the topic?

If you are assigning individual essays, you can find a quick reference to some of the ones that make these three appeals most clearly via the chart in Appendix E.

➤ Create a Shared List of Great Writer's Moves to Emulate

Students in Ms. Pandolpho's class read both adult and teenage examples of opinion writing, and, as they go, create a shared document of best practices, citing evidence from the texts. Your students might do this, too, or they might make a list of sentences or paragraphs they especially admire, which they might later use as "templates" to imitate in their own writing.

Try This:

If you began by asking students to read and answer the question, "What lessons might this essay have for your own writing?," you can now invite them to share at least one answer each publicly.

Of course, even if you're all reading the same text, answers will vary since different readers will notice different things. But here, for example, are a few "writer's moves" I admire from the essays in the section called Teenage Life Online, followed by ideas for how students could use them:

- **#1:** The way the first paragraph of "A Generation Zer's Take on the Social Media Age" sets up the tension for the whole piece: It begins with "Adults seem to think" and lists all that we older people get wrong about life on the internet, then counters that with "But if you ask any intelligent young person . . ."

  This could be a frame any student could fill in to make an argument about adult misconceptions: *"Adults seem to think . . . but if you ask any young person . . ."*
- **#2:** The use of an age-old myth as an analogy in "The Resurrection of Gilgamesh."

What comparisons can your students make to strengthen their points?

- **#3:** The honesty and vulnerability in "I'm a Disabled Teenager, and Social Media Is My Lifeline."

  What personal stories can your students tell to make a case for something important to them?
- **#4:** The way "Through the Cell Phone Camera Lens" puts us in the middle of a familiar scene—observing visitors at a gallery—and makes us see it in a new way.

  When and how can your students effectively "show" rather than "tell"?
- **#5:** The way #SelfieNation takes on the counterargument ("Due to the popularity of the selfie, older generations are labeling Generation Z as narcissistic—and apparently, selfies are to blame"), and weaves in a quote to support it before dismissing it.

  Have your students acknowledged counterarguments in their own writing? How?
- **#6:** The dramatic one-line second paragraph of "China Needs Freedom of Information": "I and my fellow 1.4 billion Chinese citizens are victims of that Wall."

  Why did this writer choose to make this line stand alone? How does that affect the essay? How might your students use a technique like this?
- **#7:** The use of extreme quotes from various social media sites to begin "Spreading Hatred is Not the Answer."

  What evidence can your students find that immediately, perhaps emotionally, makes their point?

➤ Pair These Essays with Other Texts on the Topic to Put Adult and Teen Voices in Conversation with Each Other

The 100 essays in this book take on nearly 100 different contemporary issues. Whether your class is reading adult-written fiction, nonfiction, poetry, or drama on any of these topics, you might consider pairing those texts with one from the perspective of a teenager.

For instance, many work thematically with units that are widely taught. An English class focusing on the notion of "identity" might use entries in the Gender and Sexuality or Race and Religion categories, for instance, while the section on Science, Technology, and the Environment could be read in STEM classes in tandem with adult writing on practical and ethical questions around the limits of technology or the human impact on the environment.

Some essays suggest pairings right in their titles. "Civil Obedience" (**#31**) is a play on Thoreau's "On Civil Disobedience," while "The Resurrection of Gilgamesh" (**#2**) uses that myth as a lens through which to see teen use of social media.

Many of the essays in this collection can be read together for different perspectives on the same issue. Here are just a few examples:

- Keegan Lindell and Aidan Donnelly both write about sports and concussions, but make opposing arguments (**#85** and **#86**).
- Charles Gstalder and Bhargavi Garimella each write about #MeToo, but one is from a male perspective and the other is from a female point of view (**#47** and **#54**).
- Both Miriam Gold and Kathryn Zaia write about lowering the voting age (**#37** and **#38**), but supply different reasons and advocate for it in different ways, while Ilana G. asks, "When You're Old Enough to Vote, Will You?" (**#41**).
- Three of the essays in this collection concern gun rights and policies. Daina Kalnina and Grace Scullion both make arguments based on school lockdown-drill experiences, while Paige D. writes as a gun owner herself (**#17**, **#32**, and **#39**).

Try This:

Many of these essays push back against adult perceptions of adolescent life—that social media is a danger to young people, that extreme academic stress is a normal part of growing up, that teenagers are too young and ignorant to have a voice in politics.

You might then pair some of these essays with pieces by professional opinion writers that make arguments about these same issues.

Here are some questions to ask if you do:

- Do you think teenagers see this issue differently from most adults? Why or why not?
- What insights or experiences might teenagers bring to this topic that adults might not have? What do adults bring to the discussion that teenagers can't?
- How could you make the teen argument even stronger? What other ideas and evidence might this teenage writer have included?
- What other adult writing have you read recently that might benefit from a teenage take? Why?

➤ Read This Book to Identify What's Missing

The point of this book is to inspire your students to write—to imagine their own voices and perspectives in a collection like this one, or anywhere else where they can compel a real audience.

Though the essays in the anthology were written by members of the most racially and ethnically diverse generation the United States has ever seen[5] and represent a broad range of beliefs and backgrounds, there are, of course, perspectives that are still missing, perspectives we hope future writers will supply. For example, whether because some teachers and students believe *The New York Times* is only interested in "liberal" points of view, or because Generation Z seems to be more left-leaning on social issues than some earlier generations,[6] we get far more submissions every year that could be described as liberal than conservative.

So if your students look through this collection and don't find voices that sound like theirs or issues that interest them, we hope they'll speak up. Some of our favorite submissions every year, after all, are the ones that challenge our thinking.

In a famous 1990 essay, "Windows, Mirrors and Sliding Glass Doors,"[7] the literacy scholar Rudine Sims Bishop describes the need for texts that both reflect our own lives and experiences, and texts to help us view worlds that are different from our own:

> *Books are sometimes windows, offering views of worlds that may be real or imagined, familiar or strange. These windows are also sliding glass doors, and readers have only to walk through in imagination to become part of whatever world has been created or recreated by the author. When lighting conditions are just right, however, a window can also be a mirror. Literature transforms human experience and reflects it back to us, and in that reflection we can see our own lives and experiences as part of a larger human experience. Reading, then, becomes a means of self-affirmation, and readers often seek their mirrors in books.*

While Dr. Bishop's work was centered on the need for black children to see themselves in the books they read, many have borrowed her metaphor to advocate for greater diversity in the texts we study in school in general. (In fact, in **#79**, a student uses the idea to argue we should "Let Children of Color Be Characters, Too.")

Here is a way to borrow the metaphor when considering the essays in this book.

Try This:

Ask your students:

- Which of these essays is a mirror for you, whether because it reflects something you believe, or, perhaps, because you share something important with the writer?
- Which of these essays is a window for you because it introduces you to something you didn't already know or understand or presents a perspective that challenges your thinking?
- What voices are missing from this collection? What perspectives aren't represented?

- Where might *your* voice fit in? What could you contribute to a collection like this one?

II. Finding a Topic: Helping Your Students Identify and Hone Their Own Arguments

The New York Times Learning Network has been running contests for teenagers for over a decade now, and if there's anything we've learned, it's that assignments that offer little student choice rarely result in great writing. You can spot the dutifulness from sentence one.

One of our annual contests, for example, asks kids to make connections between something they've studied in school and the world today. If a slew of essays come in that all shoehorn *To Kill a Mockingbird* into the prompt, we know the students didn't get to make their own choices about the text, and we can guess that much of what results will be fairly rote. There's little creative joy in the writing, and thus few great sentences, interesting observations, genuine questions, or original connections. There's just writing to the assignment specifications and hitting "send."

By contrast, when students choose what they want to write about, the takes, and the topics themselves, are often surprising. The voices have energy. We feel as if we're sitting next to real people as they tell us what they learned, how they learned it, and why it mattered to them. That's when we get essays that make original connections, like seeing *The Merchant of Venice* through the lens of contemporary justice reform, or showing how Newton's first two laws of physics can help explain the #MeToo movement.[8]

So how do you help your students to find the topics they care enough about to make for lively opinion writing?

➤ Ask, What Makes You Mad?

In 2017, our site did a webinar with *Times* Op-Ed columnist Nicholas Kristof. Called "Write to Change the World: Crafting Persuasive Pieces With

Help from Nicholas Kristof and the *Times* Op-Ed Page" (and still available on demand[9]), it also featured Kabby Hong, the English teacher in Wisconsin who works with our contest annually, and his student, Daina Kalnina, author of **#17**.

Mr. Kristof gave students many pieces of useful advice, much of which is woven into this Teacher's Companion. One of the first things he suggested, however: Asking yourself, "What makes you mad? What makes you angry or frustrated? What do people not get?" As he says, when writing opinion pieces, "it's good if a certain amount of passion comes through."

Mr. Hong agrees. "I haven't found a teen yet who isn't mad about something," he says.

Try This:

Invite your students to make such a list, then give them permission to write a full-out rant about any item on it. That's how at least one student in this collection found her topic. Anushka Agarwal's 2018 essay, "Civil Obedience" (**#31**), began, she says, as a "600-word rant" after an event at her school made her frustrated.

You might further free students to write as honestly as they can by telling them that no one will see this first draft. They can get their feelings down on the page knowing that it is private, then, if they choose, they can shape it for a public audience later.

➤ Or Use the Topic Generator to Help Students Brainstorm Dozens of Other Possibilities

Your students may have plenty of material if they made the list above, but the Topic Generator handout you can find in Appendix A can take them even farther.

It is a series of 16 questions (including "What makes you mad?") that can help students brainstorm scores of ideas for their own writing. The list grew out of one we posted on our site years ago, but has now been refined with the suggestions of many teachers. By design, the questions overlap somewhat; having students notice patterns in their answers is part of the point.

Try This:

You could, of course, simply photocopy the Topic Generator and hand it out for your students to finish, but perhaps a better way to work is to ask each question aloud in class, pausing to allow everyone time to write detailed answers to each.

I often started new writing units this way in my own classroom because I found that asking questions aloud slowed the pace and forced my students to think more deeply. Plus, the sound of 31 other pens scratching always seemed to encourage them to keep going long after they might have finished on their own.

I learned this technique as a new teacher one sweaty summer in the Bronx where I took my first course with the New York City Writing Project, an organization that then became my professional home for the next 18 years as I worked in NYC public schools. The strategy is what its inventor, Sondra Perl, calls "Guidelines," though I've further adapted it here.[10]

To use the Topic Generator this way, ask each question slowly, giving students time to write. But tell them before you begin that if they find themselves inspired by one of the questions and want to tune your voice out, it's fine to focus on one question alone. Your goal, after all, is to get them invested.

After students have answered the first 14 questions, pose the final two, which prompt them to loop back and review what they have written, identify just one topic to work with, and begin to break it down into possible arguments, questions, and issues.

For example, a student might have written "basketball" in answer to questions like "What are you an expert at, no matter how small?" and "What do you like to do in your free time?," but once he or she loops back and begins to explore that topic in detail, this student might add questions like, "Which player is the G.O.A.T. (greatest of all time)?"; "Should college athletes be paid?"; or "Is youth basketball getting too competitive?"

During this kind of brainstorming, some teachers share their own answers to model. Kabby Hong remembers telling one class about the fact that he was the only Asian-American in his high school and had trouble finding his place. That seemed to make many students realize they had permission to write about issues that might at first seem too personal, but which they then realized could be used to make larger, more universal points.

When you've finished asking the questions, you might have students work in partners or small groups to talk about what they discovered. However, they should remain the owners of their original writing, sharing only as much or little as they like. This isn't work to turn in so much as it is their own record to return to for ideas.

You might end the exercise with a whole-class discussion in which students can call out favorite ideas while someone takes notes. The resulting list can be surprising and inspiring—and you can suggest that students expand their individual lists to include any new ideas their classmates have suggested.

Some students, of course, just seem to know what they want to write about right away. Angela Chen, author of "Shakespeare: Friend, Not Foe" (**#76**), is one such writer. When I asked her for advice for other students, here is what she said:

> *My topic came to me fairly naturally; I think those are the best ones to follow through with, especially when you're writing an argumentative piece that requires a good bit of passion and punch.*
>
> *Fun anecdote, actually: one of my friends, when I told him about the editorial contest, made a quip something along the lines of, "Are you going to write something dweeby again? Like, we should all bend at the knee for Shakespeare or something, call him the Great Father?" He was teasing, of course, but I was like, "Dude, that is exactly what I'm going to do."*

Have a look at **#76** to see the results.

➤ **Choose from 500 Prompts for Inspiration**

Does Technology Make Us More Alone?

Who Should Decide Whether a Teenager Can Get a Tattoo or Piercing?

Should Teachers Be Armed with Guns?

Every school day since 2009 we have posed a fresh question on The Learning Network for teenagers to answer. Each one is drawn from a related *Times* article, which it both excerpts and links back to, and all are open to comment by anyone age 13 and older. We consider this public forum, which we call "Student Opinion," the most important thing we do on our site. During the busiest parts of the school year, thousands of kids from around the world post their thoughts in these public forums each month, effectively practicing argument writing for an authentic audience with each addition to the conversation.

One notable and wonderful thing about teenagers is that few of them come armed with the kinds of canned talking points that adults often do about hot-button issues. Every day we watch as students think aloud about issues in real time, often wandering back and forth across what adults might consider hard-and-fast ideological lines in order to come to their own conclusions. We also see learners at all levels in the mix, including many for whom English is not a first language. We're not looking for perfect grammar; instead, we value thoughtfulness and honesty, the willingness to take on difficult topics, and the desire to ask questions and get into conversations across divides.

On p. 83, you can find 500 of these prompts, all of which can lead to argumentative writing. If anything on The New York Times Learning Network can ever be said to have gone viral, it is the digital version of this we published several years ago. Teacher after teacher has told us how much it has helped their classes think about argumentation in general and their own stances on specific issues in particular.

And, they've told us, it's also a rich source of ideas. Amy Robinson, who teaches English in Atlanta, says, "It really helps to have models of research questions since it's hard to start from scratch. I handed your list out and my students were just fascinated. It was one of my favorite class periods, seeing them pore through the prompts and get excited."

In fact, every year we get many essays that grow directly out of these prompts. One example is **#41**, where the headline the student used, "When You Are Old Enough to Vote, Will You?," is the actual question we asked.

Try This:

Once students have found a handful of questions that interest them, they can go to our site, put in the question, and find the original piece with a link to the *Times* article that inspired it.

Because all student activities on our site are free, as are the *Times* articles they link to, it's an easy way to provide students with more context and background on an issue. If the question is still open to comment—and hundreds are—you might invite them to post on our site and practice a bit of public argument writing before they write a formal essay on the topic. (By visiting nytimes.com/column/learning-student-opinion, they can also access the many new questions that have published after this book went to press, since we post a new one each school day.)

➤ Ask, Where Do *You* Have Expertise? What Do You Know That Others Don't?

Maybe, like Eva Ferguson (**#68**), a student has an insight into the health insurance industry because she's lived with a serious health condition. Or, like Safa Saleh (**#40**) or Kevin Morales (**#45**), maybe your students have been personally affected by immigration policies and want to show others how the current system is broken.

Or maybe they've just noticed something fairly small that bugs them—that teen movies portray bullying unrealistically (**#77**), or that kids their age use language lazily (**#11**), or that, for Gen Z, "putting ourselves down is trendy" and not very healthy (**#74**).

In her book *Writing to Persuade: How to Bring People Over to Your Side,*[11] Trish Hall, a former *Times* Op-Ed page editor, writes:

> *There will always be something you know or feel or observe that others do not. We are all individuals with a singular experience and sensibility. Your writing has to reflect that, whether you are eighteen or eighty, known or unknown. (p. 45)*

She describes working with high school students in a School of *The New York Times* course on opinion writing:

> *They wanted to discuss the issues that were important to them—feminism, gay identity, Israel. I encouraged them to think about their personal singular experiences in the context of those issues. No one cares what a high school student thinks about the path to peace in the Middle East. On the other hand, if that student spent part of the summer at a camp with both Palestinian and Jewish teenagers, her recollections might led to a publishable, persuasive essay. That teenager would be telling her story, and her experience would make her an authority. (p. 46)*

It goes back to some of the questions posed on the Topic Generator (Appendix A): What are you an expert on, no matter how small? What do you get that other people just don't seem to get? What communities are you a member of? What issues are important to those communities? What aspects of your identity are most important to you? What experiences have you had in your life that have taught you a great deal?

In other words, how does your identity—however you define it—influence what you care about? What does it give you authority on and help you understand that other people can't?

All this relates to the concept of "ethos" about a subject, which I'll talk more about on p. 50, but if you or your students skim the essays in this book, you'll see that most of them make the writer's connection to the topic clear—and some that don't might be stronger if they did.

On our 2017 webinar, Nicholas Kristof talked about his own writing process, and pointed out that there's a tendency to think that the "grand issues" are more important than the "micro issues,"—but that teenagers should know the smaller issues are important, too.

"Students have expertise in the form of personal experience—sometimes bitter experiences," with issues like dating and sports, Mr. Kristof points out, and that experience gives them authority to take a stance.

Tony Xiao, the 15-year-old who wrote **#84**, about gaming, is a good example. He chose his focus because, he told me, "At the time I was writing this essay I was on winter break and I was spending 99% of my time playing games, so that's what was on my mind."

But gaming wasn't his first choice. To him, it seemed like "such an unserious topic" for a *Times* contest.

"I was thinking I should do some really bad thing, like global warming or hate speech, but when I tried to picture how my essay would go with those topics . . . I couldn't. These weren't things I thought about all the time."

His advice to other students, after being chosen as one of the top 11 winners out of 10,500 essayists?

"You have to find a topic that you care about and have experience with. I'm going to be honest: If I'd written about global warming I would have written a terrible essay."

Try This:

Invite your students to take a new piece of paper and write their topic (or claim, if they have gotten that far) in big letters. Then, have them brainstorm all the personal connections to this topic they can. This brainstorming can take the form of a list or something more visual, like a mind map.

For example, say the student who has decided to write about basketball wanted to focus on the question of whether youth teams are getting too competitive. Let's say she came up with the idea originally because she is on both a school team and a travel team and never seems to have time for anything else. In this exercise, she might write down details and memories of her own experiences, both positive and negative, but she might also write down anecdotes she has heard from teammates, parents, or coaches about, say, how much money families spend or about rising injury rates from overtraining.

As she writes, she will likely remember more and more, and one of these connections may help her focus her argument, or become a telling anecdote in her essay later, or lead her to an area of research.

If, in the process of brainstorming, any students express concern that they are focusing on issues that feel too small or too personal, or in some other way not "worthy" of being written about, they can take heart from

Nicholas Kristof. On our webinar, he told young writers never to be afraid to raise new topics.

> *"I've found that maybe my greatest power as a journalist—anybody's greatest influence as a journalist—is not just writing about the things [people] already care about, but shining a light on issues that are neglected. That's something incredibly important that op-eds can do. That kind of spotlight is the first step in getting issues addressed."*

➤ Always Connect Personal Experience to a Larger Point

Once your students have found a topic they feel personally connected to, they can open the lens wider and ask themselves, essentially, "Who cares?"

In other words, why is this something everyone should be aware of or want to do something about? What are its implications for other people, our society, and our world?

For instance, imagine if the essays in the section on Teenage Life Online were confined to the writers' individual experiences with selfies or social media and stopped there. Instead, they each go on to make arguments that relate to us all: that we can get addicted to empty validation, say; or that what can look like narcissism can actually be artistic expression and self-empowerment; or that the internet allows the disabled freedoms that we who are abled likely take for granted.

"All of us have stories to tell. The strongest ones, the ones that people will remember, often reveal something almost painfully personal even as they connect to a larger issue or story that feels both universal and urgent," says Trish Hall in *Writing to Persuade*.[12]

Bridget Smith got interested in her topic, the political divide in America, after arguments with her grandmother left her frustrated. Then, freshman year, she was on the school newspaper staff with a student who had a different set of political beliefs, and, she says, "I found it difficult to talk to him at all." But once she started exploring the topic for a possible essay, she realized there were real-world implications.

"In looking at *The New York Times* and at Pew research, the statistics about how polarized we are were so astounding. Finding those stats made the whole idea concrete for me." (Bridget's is **#30**.)

Try This:

Pose some of the questions above to your students and let them write for a minute in response: What makes your topic something other people should know and care about? What are the implications of your issue for all of us?

Then have students form small groups, or partnerships with others whose topics are related, and together discuss their answers. For example, your student who is writing about competitive youth basketball might join a group of students who are all interested in topics under the broad heading of "sports." Together they can talk about each issue and come up with reasons why they matter—to athletes as well as nonathletes, sports fans as well as those who don't know the difference between a dunk and a home run. What does each topic say about our world today? For instance, what does it mean that youth sports are getting so competitive? How might competition for spots on high-level youth teams parallel other trends or problems they see in our world?

➤ Hone a Topic into an Argument

In the spring of 2018, when Anushka Agarwal was assigned our contest for her AP Language and Composition class, the only thing she was sure of is what she *didn't* want to write about: the student walkouts happening all over the country that month in the wake of the Parkland shootings.

"I thought there were only two stances you could take—either 'Oh my god, there's so much unity' or 'Everything's bad because our school won't let us do it,'" she says.

At her school, the walkout wasn't just happening, it was hyper-planned—and not by the kids, but by the administration.

"I mean, literally the week before, there were two or three meetings every day about it, and on the day of there was an announcement like, 'At 10 a.m., don't forget to walk out of the building.' I was just feeling like, 'Wow, this really defeats the purpose,' she told me.

"Then, after the walkout my best friend and I were so frustrated. People were posting [all these uplifting] pictures on Instagram and I was thinking, 'Was I at a different event than you? That's not how it felt to me.'"

That's how Anushka found her topic and wrote the essay that would become "Civil Obedience" (**#31**).

It begins:

> *When I was five, I needed someone to hold my hand as I entered school. When I was twelve, I needed someone to point to the entrance, but I could walk in alone. Now, at sixteen, I don't need anyone—I'm a different person: independent and mature. Yet, I am treated as if I'm still a child.*

She continues:

> *. . . the administration at my school staged our protest. The day before the walkout, a minute-by-minute schedule and list of guidelines—including the only two doors we could exit from—were uploaded onto Facebook. The next day, our obedient student body shuffled into the fenced area between our school buildings only to witness teachers' comments about how "cute" we were and their apologies for being 60 seconds behind schedule. By 10:05, the end of the designated "shouting time," my friends and I lowered our posters in defeat.*

Anushka started with a "600-word rant" just after the event, then went back to edit and rewrite. It was then, she says, that she thought of Thoreau's "On Civil Disobedience" and realized she could make the connection in her title.

Anushka's story is a perfect example of finding your place in a topic. Sure, gun violence or sexism or political dysfunction may seem like terrible problems to your students—they do to most of us—but how can they stake out an argument they believe in and can substantiate within those huge topics?

A related piece of advice Nicholas Kristof shared on our webinar might help here: "Don't choose a topic, choose an argument":

> *Op-Eds work best if someone gets to the end of it and can very clearly say, "This person was arguing X." But that point has to be clear all the way through. I compare it to a bumper sticker. A column will of course be more subtle, more sophisticated, more persuasive, but it's useful if the takeaway is clear and concise in the same way as a bumper sticker is. There's a central point from which all others flow.*

Another way to think of that bumper sticker, in terms your students will understand? The thesis, or claim. Anushka's certainly passes Mr. Kristof's test that, when you finish it, you can "very clearly say, 'This person was arguing X.' " But it may surprise your students to realize that Anushka's thesis is most clearly stated not in the first paragraph but at the very end of her essay: "We need adults to accept the discomfort of us taking the reins of the gun violence movement and growing up," she writes.

Try This:

Tony Xiao, who wrote winning **#84**, knew almost from the beginning that he wanted to choose gaming as his topic . . . but what argument would he make?

Invite your students to pretend they are in the same position as Tony. How many different arguments can they come up with on the broad topic of gaming?

To start, repeat the general questions from the Topic Generator in Appendix A: "What issues are there in this topic? What are the questions, controversies, or ongoing discussions in this field?" Tell them that anything at all is legitimate inspiration for the list—arguments they've had with their parents or other adults; things they've read or heard in the media; conversations they've had with other gamers; questions or concerns they have, whether as gamers or non-gamers, themselves.

When they're done, share with them Tony's process below. He explained to me how he got from that first idea to what eventually became "Confronting Toxicity in Gaming: Going Beyond 'Mute' ":

When I chose the topic, at first I thought there weren't that many things to talk about. There was the argument you always hear that violent video games make you violent in real life, but I did some research, and there really isn't any evidence that it does, so the topic didn't seem that interesting.

But then I thought about how when I play I tend to get a lot of toxic comments because when you kill players they're not very happy about it, and when I get killed I get pretty toxic myself.

That's the angle he went with—an angle none of us on The Learning Network remember any previous student ever writing from. It was fresh, it was interesting, it was personal, yet if you read it, you'll see it is really about a much wider point that even non-gamers should know and care about.

To see how another gamer wrote about the topic, you might show students Ben C.'s essay (**#87**). Though "This is Not a Game" starts with an attention-getting personal story ("Until I lost several months of my life, I had not wanted to believe that video game addiction was real"), they will see that the piece goes on to make broad points that will be relevant to anyone who has ever struggled with a desire to escape our "dull-by-contrast world" through a screen.

➤ Make Sure Your Argument Is Focused Enough to Be Powerful

Let's say one of your students has found a topic that deeply inspires him—climate change. Thanks to a recent family trip to Miami where he was fascinated to learn how that city is planning ahead for sea-level rise, he feels personally invested, and he thinks it should be easy to find some research showing how pressing the problem is, not just for Floridians, but for all of us.

Now imagine how many essays we get every year on the broad problem of the human impact on our environment. Teenagers are passionate about it and worry that other generations aren't doing enough to address the problem. Unfortunately, many use their 450 words to rehash broad arguments they just don't have the room to argue well. Plus, we've read better versions somewhere else, written by scientists or policy experts with far more expertise.

These kinds of student essays often begin something like this:

> *Climate change is a change in global or regional climate patterns, in particular a change apparent from the mid to late 20th century onwards and attributed largely to the increased levels of atmospheric carbon dioxide produced by the use of fossil fuels. It is the most important issue of our time because it affects us all. Climate change is devastating our earth, and we must find solutions.*

In other words, they often start with a definition taken directly from an internet source, then move on to a claim so broad it could take thousands of words to defend meaningfully.

To explain to your students the difference between those generic essays and more effective ones, have them read some of the pieces in this collection that take a piece of a problem rather than tackling it all—yet leave us caring about the big picture, anyway.

To start, if your students haven't yet read "Nothing Gets Between Me and My Sushi . . . Except Plastic, Maybe" (**#62**), they might look at it from this perspective now. In this essay, 15-year-old Sophia Lee, an "Asian-American self-proclaimed millennial foodie," takes us through her horrified discovery that, because the ocean is full of plastic, so, likely, is the fish she eats:

> *There's so much plastic in the water, churned down to the size of rice grains or smaller, and fish gobble it up. When the fish end up on our dinner plates, guess what? Our bellies receive an unsettling supplement that wasn't on the menu.*

Sophia makes it personal and small enough to explore in the confines of the word count. She does it in a friendly, playful voice that makes you want to learn from her. In zooming in on her personal problem, and then out to contextualize it by giving us facts about plastics in our diet and how they affect us, she makes the problem tangible, even visceral, and gives us strong motivation to heed her call to action. (Indeed, I'll admit that since I read the essay myself, I've been rigorous about carrying a reusable bag wherever I go, something none of the hundreds of other essays I'd read on the topic, by adults as well as students, ever motivated me to do consistently.)

If your students check out the chapter on science and the environment, they'll find two additional examples. "Climate Literacy: A Critical Step Toward Climate Stability" (**#63**) focuses on school curriculum, and "Paper or Plastic? How about a Paper ON Plastic!" (**#67**) looks at excessive packaging. Like Sophia's essay, they are immediate and concrete.

Or let's take another complex topic that students write passionately about for our contest every year: race and racism. You can find race-related issues woven into essays throughout the Student Voice collection, in chapters on School as well as on Civic Life and Politics, but our Race and Religion chapter highlights a handful of powerful pieces in which it is a central focus. Here are two examples.

Matteo Wong uses his essay, "The Asian Misnomer: What the Affirmative Action Debate Misses" (**#56**), to spotlight just one small detail, but one that speaks volumes on the topic of diversity. Here is his first paragraph:

> *One Scantron bubble and five letters: "Asian." That's all the College Board needs to encompass the heritage of thousands of students and 48 countries. Those five letters are also what many college admissions officers use as the basis for establishing diversity through affirmative action. While some institutions provide options such as "Chinese," "Asian Indian" and "Other Asian," a glance at official demographics reports shows that they don't actually care; all of these ethnicities are still homogenized as Asian.*

And in "The Missing Anthropological Exhibit at the Museum of Natural History" (**#61**), Alec Farber chooses one museum to illustrate the way our culture centers a white, Western worldview. He argues that an institution with exhibits that include a Hall of Asian Peoples and a Hall of African Peoples needs to also include a Hall of European Peoples:

> *The idea of more European culture in our institutions can sound unnecessary, and even racist, to many. But before judging, ask yourself: What are*

the consequences of portraying Europeans as above anthropology? When only people of color are exhibited in the museum, visitors learn that there must be something intrinsically different about European culture. The exhibits teach this because they are rooted in a white, 19th century worldview. Although updated, the exhibits still reflect a time when European artifacts were considered "art" or "history," while other artifacts were labeled "natural history." The museum's European superiority was so extreme that, in 1897, six Eskimos were displayed solely as "a source of amusement" for visitors. Such racism in anthropology was common at a time when anything European was considered "civilization," while anything else was labeled "primitive."

Try This:

If your students have access to the entire anthology, they might look through the chapter on gender to see examples of how individual students have found their place in the larger conversation, another on which we regularly receive hundreds of entries.

- "Why I, a Heterosexual Teenage Boy, Want to See More Men in Speedos" isn't the only essay to take on gender stereotypes and expectations. In "Egghead Son vs. Airhead Daughter?" (**#55**), Rachel S. and Nancy B. focus on how parents raise sons and daughters differently, while "You Don't Need to Glitter Things Pink to Get Me into STEM" (**#51**) talks back to the gendered marketing materials one young woman received from engineering programs.
- Some essays spotlight aspects of womanhood that the authors feel need to be rethought. In "The Red Stain on Society" (**#46**), Holly Keaton explores why periods need to be discussed, normalized, and understood as "simply another function of the human body." And in "Redefining Ladylike" (**#48**), Zoie Taylore looks at the female habit of apologizing too often—what she calls "the 'sorry' epidemic"—to show how it can keep women from speaking their minds.
- Two essays concern the #MeToo movement. One is by a teenage boy who says he and his friends long for nuanced education on "what constitutes reprehensible behavior." The other is by a young woman who

is a survivor of child sexual assault herself, and says the movement allowed her to share her experiences after years of silence. She calls for "changes to laws and policies that perpetuate the imbalance of power between men and women" (**#9** and **54**).

- Finally, two essays invite us to think about gender from new points of view. In "Under Black Cloaks" (**#53**), Bincheng Mao, who spent two years living in Dubai and Qatar, describes why she finds Saudi gender policies "dehumanizing." And in "The Question Up For Debate: Is Feminism Really For Everyone?" (**#52**), Nico Mayer argues that we need "a broader representation of feminism than what mainstream media has provided" and introduces the notion of intersectionality.

➤ Understand the Range of "Takes" Others Have Already Expressed on the Issue

Not only are there general topics like climate change that appear in essay after essay every year of our contest, but there are also always one or two specific news stories that dominate submissions every spring because of their relevance to young people. In 2018 it was the Parkland shooting and #MeToo, in 2019 it was the college admissions scandal, and in 2020 it was, of course, the coronavirus pandemic.

But if everyone is writing about these things, how can your students say something new?

Try This:

New Jersey teacher Amanda Lentino suggests showing students how a broad topic can inspire a huge range of "takes" by putting that topic into a search engine along with the word "opinion" and seeing what results.

For example, when Ms. Lentino's students tried the technique with the terms "college scandal opinion" in March of 2019, the exercise showed them quickly how many different ideas there were on what the scandal was "really about."

To some pundits it showed a national misunderstanding of the true purpose of a college education. To others it was more of an indictment of how society is rigged for the rich. For still others it was about how we overvalue the Ivy League, or how we place too much emphasis on college sports, or how we Americans are corrupted by greed, or . . . the list went on.

But if your students are writing about something that "everyone" seems to have an opinion on, they should also know that it might be impossible to take a completely original stance. Instead, they can remember some of the earlier advice in this guide and ground what they want to argue in specifics that make their personal point of view on the issue tangible and memorable.

For example, the one piece on the college admissions scandal that made it to the final round in 2019 is **#24**. Maria Olifer's angle is evident in her title: "I'm Not Surprised at the College Admissions Scandal, and You Shouldn't Be Either." She begins with an engaging description of what her school lunchroom was like the day the news broke, then segues into how being a senior applying to colleges gives her a window into how "avenues of college acceptance" are often "paved with the power of the American dollar."

It was the best of the many we received, not because the writer made an original point—many people said the same thing right after the scandal broke—but because of how she made us experience the financial specifics:

> *This year, I applied to 11 universities. Each university had an application fee averaging $80. I had to pay to take the ACT ($62 per attempt, 2 attempts) and the Advanced Placement (AP) exam ($94 per exam, 13 exams); for each prep book that I used to study; and then again to send these scores to colleges.*

Finally, if there was ever a time when it might have felt difficult to say something original about a topic, it was the spring of 2020, when the whole planet seemed focused on the same thing—the coronavirus pandemic. As the contest submission period stretched through March and April, we worried that we'd receive 8,000 essays that would become a Covid-19 blur for our judges. But we shouldn't have been concerned: a glance at just the first 50 made it clear that the impact of the pandemic on the lives of teenagers was so profound and wide-ranging that finding individual and memorable "ways in" had been no problem at all.

Some students focused on the social justice issues the pandemic made stark, writing about racism and xenophobia, income inequality, prison reform, hunger, homelessness, voting rights, the digital divide, and more. Others found new questions to think about, from the rights of frontline workers to the problem of toilet-paper hoarding. Students from countries around the globe focused on the politics of the pandemic, analyzing how their governments were handling the crisis.

But we were especially impressed by all the ways students found to make the personal universal. Hundreds of essayists found larger arguments in their individual experiences of loneliness and anxiety; their disappointment in missing proms and graduations; their changing relationships with parents, siblings, friends, and teachers; and the books, movies, music, and video games that kept them occupied for weeks in quarantine.

We were still judging the spring 2020 contest as these books went into production, so none of those essays appear among the 100 in the Student Voice collection. Instead, we added an appendix with three excellent representative pieces, and by the time you read this you'll be able to find many more on our site. As with Maria Olifer's essay on the college admissions scandal above, we didn't choose these essays because they made points no one else thought of, we chose them because they made those points in original, specific, and elegant ways.

➤ Make Sure Your Argument Fits Your Intended Audience and Purpose

If your students are on social media, they're already practiced in how to craft messages for real audiences and purposes. Without realizing it, they're naturals at the rhetorical situations they encounter communicating on Instagram or TikTok or Twitter or anywhere else they spend a lot of time. They are careful to use the language—the hashtags, memes, and in-jokes—of the communities they care about in ways that that community values.

As Grant Wiggins put it, "In real-world writing, 'audience' and 'purpose' are not mere buzzwords; they are task-defining: the consequences of your writing matter for a specific audience in a specific situation."[13]

For whom are your students writing their opinion pieces? What would they like to have happen as a result? For much of what students compose in school, the answers to these questions are a given: "my teacher" and "to get a good grade." Your students may never have had to think beyond that. But if they are sending their opinion pieces out into the world, answers to questions like where they're sending it, who will be reading it, and what they hope to accomplish will affect many of their choices.

Jennifer Fletcher, author of *Teaching Arguments*, says it another way: "When real writers write for work or publication, they make a close study of successful models of writing in their chosen area to see what passes muster with a given discourse community."[14]

Of course, the essays in this collection all had the same first audience—our contest judges—and were written, presumably, for the same purpose: to meet the criteria on our rubric as well as possible in order to win. But they all have to work for a general audience once they are published, and students who do not think sufficiently about audience don't make it to the final round.

For instance, one of the essays we got in 2019 mocked "older people" for not understanding internet culture. It devoted a whole first paragraph to listing all the things that we olds (defined as people over 40) could not possibly get about social media and its nuances.

The problem? The first hurdle in this contest was impressing our dozens of judges. Many of us are over 40, and most of us like to think of ourselves as being fairly fluent in internet culture. Moreover, the examples this student used to illustrate the point were all fairly mainstream, something most well-read adults of any age would recognize and understand. While such an argument might work to entertain fellow teenagers, this kid had clearly misjudged the audience they needed to reach first. We didn't buy the argument since we were all living counterarguments.

On the other hand, we are impressed every year by those students who show a sophisticated understanding of how to speak to an audience effectively.

Every writer has to ask themselves, What will my readers already know? What can I assume and what should I spell out? But every year we get many submissions from students in China and South Korea, and the best of those make it clear that the writers have pitched their arguments specifically to an American audience. They gracefully gloss details about aspects of their countries or cultures that Americans will need to understand to appreciate their points, and many of them also make comparisons to American culture to further bridge the divide.

A good example is **#23**, "The Korean Dream Is a Korean Nightmare," which opens with a dramatic first paragraph that brings home to an outsider just how seriously that country takes its college admissions test. It then goes on to compare the test to the American SAT, as well as to the Canadian college admissions system. Any student reading this piece from anywhere in the world would come away understanding something about how the three systems work.

"Fairness in Education: The Upper-Class Monopoly on Resources" (**#26**), similarly looks at the system in China, but begins by likening it to U.S. college admissions, and explains key context about the Chinese education system and its history.

Alissa Warren, an eighth grade teacher in Denver, invites her students to submit to our contest as part of a larger argument unit for which they must also make websites about their issues. In 2019, one student's argument was that LeBron James was the reason for the Lakers' failure that season. "The drama he has brought to the team is detrimental," this student claimed.

Ms. Warren has her class break down the rhetorical situation before they start writing. Who is your intended audience? Who, therefore, are you as the speaker? What is the subject? What's the occasion? What's your impetus for doing this? What do you want to get out of it?

On his website, the student wrote as an athlete and fan speaking to other athletes and fans, and he used a great deal of basketball-specific vocabulary and evidence to make his case. Doing so showed his credibility with the subject and was completely appropriate for the "discourse community" to whom he was speaking. But when he needed to take that argument and turn it into an essay for our contest, his audience changed. He could no longer assume his readers would know terms like "defensive rebound percentage"—so, instead, he skipped some, defined others, and used more general examples instead.

Try This:

Have students choose an essay, whether from this collection or one of their own, and imagine a different or more specialized audience for it. What would need to change? Why?

For instance, how would "The N.H.L. Should Do Away With Fighting" (**#90**) have to be recast for an audience of rabid hockey fans? How might some of the essays in the Civic Life and Politics section be different if students were writing not for *The New York Times*, but for a site that is more extreme politically, whether to the right or the left? How would the pieces in the section on Science, Technology, and the Environment morph if they were written for STEM experts rather than for a lay audience?

III. Getting Beyond the Echo Chamber: Researching for a Range of Viewpoints

> *The scenario is familiar: A well-meaning teacher delves into a research unit by asking their students to self-select topics that pique their curiosity. The teacher then asks them to choose a side, stake a claim, and seek out relevant evidence to support it.*
>
> *What might not be so obvious, however, is the hidden curriculum of this assignment, which reinforces the idea that authentic research involves little more than locating ideas that cement what students already hold to be true.*

So begins a piece for The Learning Network written by Jacqueline Hesse and Christine McCartney,[15] the two teachers in Newburgh, New York, who invited me into their classroom as the 2018–19 school year ended. Several months earlier, they had written for us about how they had taken a new approach to doing research that had helped their students include a much wider variety of viewpoints.

For many teachers, helping students learn to get beyond a simple pro/con, black-and-white view of complex issues is an important goal. Teachers will always be in a uniquely powerful position to help young people learn how to talk to each other across divides, but supporting civil conversation in the classroom in today's overheated political climate feels to many increasingly urgent.

And if submissions to our contest are a good indication of what's on the minds of Gen Z, it's safe to say that our political polarization plagues them, too. Since 2016, student after student has written about the poisonous effects of shouting past each other instead of learning to listen—none better than Bridget Smith in her piece "Dinner Table Politics" (**#30**). As she writes, "If we can't talk about the issues, how can we fix them?"

Kevin Tang makes a similar argument in "I CAN'T HEAR YOU: Echo Chambers in America" (**#42**): "When we surround ourselves only with ideas that are similar to our own, we succumb to groupthink as we take everything we read as fact. This dangerous cycle perpetuates disinformation since we almost always don't take the time to independently verify what we read and view to be true."

This section details a way to use the research process to help students immerse themselves deeply in big questions about our world—not to find a "right answer" or to narrowly support one point of view, but to unpack an issue fully, ask questions, hear from many sides, ask more questions, and ultimately reason their own way to a nuanced stance.

➤ Begin by Getting Beyond Your "Filter Bubble" and Finding a Range of Credible Sources

Where and how do your students get their news and opinion now? How much comes via social media feeds? How diverse is that feed in terms of demographic details like the ages, races, religions, geographical locations, interests, and political affiliations of the people they follow? Do your students, like many adults, live in "filter bubbles" where they see only news, information, and opinions that conform to and reinforce their own beliefs?

Not only is the pace of information today relentless, but fewer and fewer of us seem able to even agree on what's true and what's fabricated. Teaching teenagers how to research offers an invitation to help them learn how to navigate information competently and critically at the same time.

In her book *Being the Change*, the teacher and writer Sara K. Ahmed points out that learning about what's in your students' news feeds offers another opportunity as well. It's a chance to get to know them better, to see how they make sense of the world and to undertstand how the information that matters to them connects to their identities.[16]

Back in 2017, The Learning Network ran a media literacy contest that challenged teenagers to examine their daily "news diets" and figure out how to make them more well-balanced. We suggested a three-step process, which you can find detailed in a lesson plan on our site.[16] Part of our goal was to get students to think about information consumption not just as a school assignment, but in the context of their real lives, since, as we had noticed ourselves in writing lesson plans on the topic, quick classroom fixes for countering the "fake news" problem didn't ever seem to do enough.

Several hundred teenagers participated, and wrote essays or made short videos about what they discovered.[18] Max Wilson, 16, spoke for many of them when he wrote,

> *Examining, logging, and changing my media diet has been an incredibly eye-opening process. Just like the products at your average fast food joint, my media diet was composed of four low quality ingredients in different combinations—bias, selective reporting, out-of-context quotes, and irrelevant purposes.*

Most of the students who did the challenge reported realizing that they followed mostly sources that confirmed their own views. Jenna V., 17, wrote that she was dismayed by the fact that almost all the news sources and individuals she followed were liberal—most "very, very liberal."

Nicole Duerr, 14, had the same problem, but from the opposite point of view:

> *Why did I never consider what the liberal news outlets had to say? I realized that I rejected liberal news because I didn't want to know their narrative. I was grounded in my own views, and stubbornly rejected whatever the left-wing had to say.*

Sarah Gross, a humanities teacher in New Jersey who often begins class by having her students read an article from that day's print *New York Times*, says she's consumed by the problem.

> *I sometimes feel like a majority of my ninth graders are getting their "news" from conspiracy-theory stuff on YouTube. At home and in school, we adults focus on things like "Don't share your private info online"—but they're way, way beyond that. The answer is not saying, Wikipedia and Reddit are not credible sources. We need to teach them to read everything critically. My 13- and 14-year-olds have been on Fortnite and browsing Reddit since they were 10, but they haven't read a newspaper, for the most part, until they sit down in my class.*

As your students go through the process of learning to write better opinion essays, you might talk with them about their information diets and help broaden them by finding reliable sources—websites, books, newspapers, magazines, radio, TV, podcasts, and interviews with real, live people—that introduce them to a variety of perspectives on the issues they care about. Nonpartisan sites like livingroomconversations.org and https://allsidesforschools.org/ might be good places to start.

Try This:

If our three-part News Diet Challenge is too elaborate for the time you have, you might come at it by having your students read and discuss one of the essays in this collection.

Jeffrey W.'s "Journalistic Objectivity Was Yesterday's Saving Grace" (**#44**) describes the media landscape we live in today and outlines his opinion as to why it is dangerous. Invite them to read and annotate it, having a conversation with it on paper. What lines resonate with their own experiences? Where does the writer make the most interesting points? What might they add or argue with? What implications do his words have for their own lives?

➤ Understand What It Means to Enter the "Unending Conversation"

Many who teach argument-writing use literary theorist Kenneth Burke's metaphor of the "unending conversation" as an effective way to help students understand how to think of their own role in academic discourse:

> *Imagine that you enter a parlor. You come late. When you arrive, others have long preceded you, and they are engaged in a heated discussion, a discussion too heated for them to pause and tell you exactly what it is about. In fact, the discussion had already begun long before any of them got there so that no one present is qualified to retrace for you all the steps that had gone before. You listen for a while until you decide that you have caught the tenor of the argument; then you put in your oar. Someone answers; you answer him; another comes to your defense; another aligns himself against you, to either the embarrassment or gratification of your opponent, depending upon the quality of your ally's assistance. However, the discussion is interminable. The hour grows late, you must depart. And you do depart, with the discussion still vigorously in progress.*[19]

In other words, listen to all sides before joining in—and know that you'll be adding just one perspective to a discussion that began before you and will continue after you. Understand that any issue important enough to research and write about is complicated, and no one person has "the answer."

Try This:

Here are two quick ways to show students how a digital version of an "unending conversation" can look.

- The Letters to the Editor or comments section of a newspaper article on a controversial topic can help students quickly see a range of opinion about an issue and help them realize that a published piece, no matter how authoritative the author, is not the final word on a topic.

  The essays in this book are of course, also part of this larger conversation. Your students might choose the ones that are on topics they are also writing about and "talk back" to them in the same way. Where is this student writer off base? Where is the logic of the argument faulty? What evidence or counterargument might he or she be ignoring?

- A *Times*-specific resource, one long beloved by teachers, is Room for Debate (RFD), a feature the Opinion section ran from 2009–17. Though it has been discontinued, the discussions are mostly evergreen, and a full archive of them is available online.[2]

  Each Room for Debate post takes an issue or event in the news and rounds up opinions on it from four to six knowledgeable outside contributors. Because each contributor posts only a brief, four- or five-paragraph response, and because the design of the feature makes it easy to quickly grasp how the viewpoints differ, it is especially accessible to students.
- Have your students scan a list of the forums, which range from big "essential" questions like "Is the U.S. is still a 'land of opportunity'?" to everyday practical and ethical questions like, "Is it okay to sell store-bought items at bake sales?" Then, show them how the student writer of **#57**, "Muddying a Sacred Cloth," wove in details from one of them as evidence in her essay on Muslim women and the hijab.

  Students might observe, too, how each of the RFD responders do what we've recommended earlier in this guide: focus on just one aspect of the larger issue, writing from their own personal position of authority. For example, four people respond to the question "Should every young athlete get a trophy?" including a high school and a college athlete, a manufacturer of trophy parts, and a bestselling author of books related to the topic, but each grounds their contribution in one specific area of expertise.[20]

➤ Research to Understand a Range of Perspectives

Let's say that your students, like those in Jacqueline Hesse and Christine McCartney's class, are discussing the ongoing controversy that begin in 2016 after football player Colin Kaepernick knelt in protest during the National Anthem.

These teachers borrow a strategy of the Capital District Writing Project educator Christopher Mazura and ask their students to place their claims along a continuum, with opposing beliefs at each end.

One end, then, might read "Professional athletes should stand for the national anthem, regardless of their political beliefs," while the opposite might say, "Athletes should be able to choose not to stand during the national anthem as a peaceful expression of their political beliefs" at the other. "After new ideas or articles they encounter, students reposition their claims and articulate how and why their thinking has shifted," the teachers write.

Ms. Hesse and Ms. McCartney described in their piece for us how their students go on to use the continuum in their own research[22]:

> *After workshopping possible topics as a whole class, students work in pairs and, later, larger groups to comment on one another's ideas for research and to articulate their tentative stances toward their chosen topics. Here, students begin to plot their claims along their aforementioned continuums. This process also helps students to begin exploring a range of counterclaims.*
>
> *After this initial research phase, most students are eager to reconsider and replot their stances on their continuums. We ask that students reflect in writing about why their claims are or are not shifting or deepening.*
>
> *We have found that students experience freedom when they realize that, in their final papers, they don't have to prove something they no longer believe after conducting research.*

A related idea comes from Erica Lee Beaton, a tenth grade teacher in Cedar Springs, Michigan, who teaches what she calls "arguments that listen."

Every year, her English department requires that each student write an argumentative research essay, and, just like Ms. Hesse and Ms. McCartney, every year she notices that, without her intervention, students tend to write one-sided arguments that acknowledge other points of view only glancingly in order to dismiss them.

Instead, she has reimagined the assignment to make looking for commonalities and "humanizing the other side" a crucial element.

As her students research their topics, they go through a number of exercises that ensure that they read "through two lenses," always giving equal weight to the opposing point of view and seeking to understand why others might feel the way they do. For instance, early on she has them research answers to questions like these:

- What kinds of people might be on "this side" of your issue? What types of people might be on "that side"?
- What kinds of experiences might have brought them to "this side"? What kinds of experiences might have brought them to "that side"? (The handout reminds students to consider categories of experience like social, cultural, economic, racial, historical, geographical, religious, and political.)
- Keeping these experiences in mind, what does Group X value? What does Group Y value? What does each group care about? What is important to each?

Exercises like this, she says, help her students move from stereotypes about the other side to "a place of better understanding."

Another of the tools Ms. Beaton uses to show her students what true "listening arguments" might look like is the YouTube series Middle Ground.[23] This series "explores the beliefs of people holding opposing political and religious views" by inviting small groups on two sides of an issue to sit down and have productive conversations. Over multiple seasons, it has featured conversations between pro-life and pro-choice advocates, athiests and Christians, cops and ex-felons, and Palestinians and Israelis. Ms. Beaton says once she introduces the series, she can't get her kids to stop watching them, so fascinated are they by how these different kinds of strangers begin to understand each other. "They come in and say, 'I just watched four or five last night,'" she says.

Like the Newburgh students, Ms. Beaton's students often shift their beliefs after research. For example, she described one student, a boy who came to class the first day with his topic "ready to go."

"He just said, 'I'm writing about abortion' and put his headphones on—giving me that nonverbal 'leave me alone,' " she remembers.

But as this boy went through the steps of the "listening argument," he had to consider the views of the other side—in his case, someone who was pro-choice. Meanwhile, there were two other students in the class who were also writing essays on abortion, one from pro-life perspective and the from a pro-choice stance. As they each researched separately, Ms. Beaton says, all three felt the need to discuss what they were finding. "They came to me and said, 'Can we just go out into the hall and talk?' "

Soon after that, about two weeks into the project, this boy approached her.

"He said, 'I need some help. I'm changing my topic. I'm starting over.' He said he had been researching at home, looking at what the government does to support mothers with unexpected pregnancies. So I asked, 'What did you find?' And he had this look on his face of surprise and he said, 'We don't do much!' "

Ms. Beaton says he realized he needed to change his claim—and as he described why, he unconsciously used the metaphor of a continuum of belief:

> *He said, "I know I was over here, that abortion should be illegal"—and here he gestured to one side of the room—"but now I want to move over here"—here he gestured toward the middle of the room. He said, "I think the government should still make it illegal, but I want to argue that they should do more to support pregnant mothers. I'm not changing my mind that abortion is wrong, but this is what I think now."*

Meanwhile, the student who was pro-choice? She, too, came to a different position after conversations with her classmates. Ms. Beaton says she began to realize that the heart of the conflict is defining when life begins, and her writing started to thoughtfully recognize why many think life begins at conception. In the end, her essay focused on the societal impasse over this question, a much more nuanced position than the "scrappy and somewhat combative stance" she initially took when the trio began their small-group discussions.

Only one essay in this collection takes on abortion, and this writer, too, comes at the issue not by arguing whether it is right or wrong, but by proposing a way to mitigate the problem. Like Ms. Beaton's student, Sylvia Hollander acknowledges the impasse. Her essay (**#22**) begins, "Abortion is one of the most polarizing topics in the United States. For many on both sides, you're either with them or against them, and unwilling to compromise."

Try This:

To help your students move from a rigid "pro/con" view of their issue toward more of a nuanced continuum of ideas, you might do an all-class version of the "barometer" exercise.

In it, students literally show where they stand on an issue by placing themselves physically on an imaginary line across the classroom. On one end is "strongly agree," while "strongly disagree" is on the other, with the full continuum in between. Students can volunteer to articulate why they placed themselves on various points on the line, and, as they listen to other students' arguments, can reposition themselves as they like.

Some of the lighter topics in our 500 prompts for argumentative writing might be a good place to start. For instance, you might begin with a statement like, "It's better to be neat than messy," "Manners are important" or "Prom is not worth it" to help your students get comfortable articulating their stances and listening to each other's reasoning.

IV. Composing and Revising: Tackling The Elements of an Argument Essay

So, how do your students bring all this together to write something original and interesting? And what can these 100 successful essays teach your students as they go?

As with all the advice in this Teacher's Companion, you and your students can use what follows in any order. Writing, after all, is really rewriting, and different students will need help with different elements of their work at different times. And at this point, your students may have a great deal of writing already, and their biggest challenge may be shaping it.

If there is one essay I think every teacher of writing should read, it's "Making Meaning Clear: The Logic of Revision," a 1981 piece by the Pulitzer Prize-winning journalist and English professor, Donald Murray.[24] First introduced to me by the New York City Writing Project that long-ago summer in the Bronx, it is a piece I return to whenever I am writing something difficult myself. Here is how it begins:

> *The writer's meaning rarely arrives by room-service, all neatly laid out on the tray. Meaning is usually discovered and clarified as the writer makes hundreds of small decisions, each one igniting a sequence of consideration and reconsideration. Revision is not just clarifying meaning, it is discovering meaning and clarifying it while it is being discovered. That makes revision a far more complicated process than is usually thought—and a far simpler process at the same time. It is complicated because the writer cannot just go to the rule book. Revision is not a matter of correctness, following the directions in a manual. The writer has to go back again and again and again to consider what the writing means and if the writer can accept, document, and communicate that meaning. In other words, writing is not what the writer does after the thinking is done; writing is thinking.*

If your students have come this far—if they have found an argument they care about making, done some informal writing to get initial ideas on the page, and tested and deepened their claim with research—it's time for them to take Donald Murray's advice. He emphasizes that it is "the student, not the teacher, who decides what writing means," and reminds writers at any level that "if I listen to my own developing voice . . . I will discover what I have to say."

Here are many ways to do that, with help from the winning essays to give your students ideas for each element.

➤ Before Writing, Pull Back and Look at the Big Picture

Before your students begin to compose their final pieces, they might take a step back and look at what they have. Many teachers confer individually with students at this point, and I spoke to Kabby Hong just as he was doing so with his students in 2019.

"I try to talk to every single kid and build in time. You can tell when the kid has picked the right topic. There's an energy to that conversation. The process is like cooking, and you can't cook without heat. If you don't have emotional heat, you'll just have ingredients. My conversation with them is to see if they have any heat. If they do, we're good and we can go from there," he says.

Another strategy to try? Asking students to write about their progress.

Try This:

As she wrote about in an essay for The Learning Network,[25] Beth Pandolpho, a language arts teacher in New Jersey, has her students finish these sentence-starters:

- My topic is . . .
- It matters because . . .
- I am personally concerned about it because . . .
- My main argument in one sentence is . . .
- People should care about this issue because . . . and I will make them care by . . .
- I think the primary opposing viewpoint is . . .
- In response to this viewpoint, I will likely say . . .
- As a result of reading my editorial, I think people should do/think/feel . . .

The National Writing Project, which invites young people to "enter into public conversation about questions that matter to them" via its Civically Engaged Curriculum,[26] poses this series of useful questions:

- Who is my audience and what is my purpose?

- How do I establish my voice as one worth listening to and engaging with?
- What choices in language are appropriate for my intended audience and purposes?
- How do I establish the issue's importance?
- How do I articulate why [the position] I advocate is reasonable and feasible?
- What evidence, stories, and reasoning most effectively support my position?

At this point in the process, how easy is it for your students to finish these sentences or answer these questions?

➤ "Start with a Bang"

Take it from those of us who read thousands of student essays for this contest every year: the first line tells your audience more than you imagine. When a student gives up that key real estate to something dull or clichéd, it's hard to recover.

If they are writing a 450-word opinion piece, sentences like "This essay will look at why we need better gun control laws," are a waste of space. We shouldn't need to be told; we should already realize what the piece will be about from the headline, or from something in the introduction that *shows* it.

On the webinar he did with us, Nicholas Kristof advised students to "start with a bang," and told a story about being a young reporter at the *Times* in the 1980s, writing then about economics. As he'd take the subway to work in the morning, he would look around the train and see people reading the paper—and he'd wait eagerly for them to get to his piece. Some of them, of course, would ignore it completely, but others would stop.

"Maybe they'd read a paragraph or two and then you'd just see their eyes move on, or they'd turn the page . . . and you'd want to grab them and say, 'I've got this incredible 18th paragraph!' Of course, that doesn't work. You're competing for a scarce resource, and that's people's attention," he said.

Try This:

Here are four first sentences from essays in this collection:

I used to not want to be Asian. (#10)

One day after school, I ran into the kitchen and saw the breaking news crack my sturdy mother. (#32)

On a frigid night in the midst of Michigan's polar vortex, I found myself stranded in a grocery store parking lot with an unchangeable flat tire. (#36)

A skirt on Zara. A Dior campaign. Keziah Daum's prom dress. What do all of these things have in common? They are the latest victims of America's politically correct crusaders. (#100)

Ask your students if these openings pull them into a scene, a story, a setting, or an argument and make them want to read on. For instance, how do they react to *"I used to not want to be Asian"*? Where do they think the essay might go from that line?

If your students have access to the full anthology, have them look through and identify their own favorite openings, then analyze why and how they worked. For example, what do they think of the first lines of "Redefining Ladylike," #48?

Then, have them choose one or more as templates for their own writing. They might read the results aloud when they're finished.

➤ Why This and Why You?: Personal Authority, or *Ethos*, as Evidence

On p. 22, we have already discussed how part of the process of helping students figure out what to write about is thinking about where they have expertise—what they know that others may not. But now you may need to convince them that that experience—their personal stories, or observations as a stakeholder on an issue—is actually *evidence*.

Every writer in this collection is a teenager, and thus every writer has the built-in ethos of speaking about how their issue concerns people their own age. Perhaps that's why the School section is our lengthiest. Those essays are often strikingly passionate, detailed, and well-argued, because the authority of having lived the problem is clear in every line.

In that section, you'll see especially vivid examples of students putting the readers in their shoes, describing everyday high school scenarios and making us see them anew. For example, take a look at the opening of "Inferior Substitute Teaching" (**#27**), which describes a scene that anyone who has ever been to school has experienced, but does so in service of showing just how big a waste of time bad subbing can be.

As they read, your students may start to notice that the strongest essays in all sections are those that come with a built-in answer to the questions we asked earlier: "Why this and why you?" For example, Narain Dubey begins his "Breaking the Blue Wall of Silence: Changing the Social Narrative About Policing in America" (**#92**) this way:

> *As a child, I thought of police officers with veneration—if I saw a cop in the park, I felt safer. I told myself that when I got older, I would be wearing the badge too.*
>
> *At 12 years old, I learned about police brutality. When I first saw the video of Eric Garner being thrown to the ground by police officers, I thought it was a movie. Despite knowing that the officers were at fault, I refused to change my internal rhetoric; I thought the media was only portraying the bad side of the people I saw as heroes.*
>
> *Then on July 31, 2017, a police officer shot and killed my cousin, Isaiah Tucker, while he was driving. Isaiah wasn't just my cousin. He was also a young, unarmed, African-American man. I no longer dreamt of becoming a police officer.*

Narain says that, from the start, he wanted to find a topic that he could "talk about genuinely and from my own life, rather than just researching and regurgitating what I found online." But he also struggled:

> *Part of me debated whether or not I should respect privacy and keep my story within the family. But everyone has to notice that [police shootings of young black men] is an issue, and I saw I could use my experience to explain this situation on a larger scale. I just wanted to make sure I did it a respectful way. I didn't want to sound like I was exploiting it. And I actually saw writing about it as an opportunity to process what happened for myself as well.*

There are many essays like Narain's, essays that are hard to read, but that are unforgettable because the student was brave enough to take their own experience and use it to call for change. The piece that follows his in this collection is headlined, "Rape: The Only Crime Where Victims Have to Explain Themselves" (**#93**), and we learn in the first paragraphs that the author herself has been raped—and then discovered, after reporting it to the police, how few rapists are ever prosecuted. As Corinne Ahearn writes in her final line, "Shocking? It should be." Ask your students how these essays might have been different if Corinne and Narain had left their own experiences off the page.

Yet effective ethos, or authority about a subject, does not have to come as a result of a harrowing experience. Stephanie Zhang found her topic after a lifetime of being lined up in alphabetical order in school and always being placed last (**#19**). Zahra Nasser uses her childhood observations about her mother's hijab to puzzle through her own take on a complicated issue (**#57**). And in "Am I Dangerous?," Paige D. begins by describing her own prowess with a gun to argue her point that logic, not anecdotes, should drive the debate over gun safety (**#39**).

Sometimes students leave their own stake in an argument out of an editorial that is crying out for it. For example, if a student is writing about raising the minimum wage and he works at a local fast-food business alongside adults for whom that wage is their sole income, it is likely he has a story, an image, or a quote from that experience that can make his point memorable. If another student is writing about body image, including the fact that she is a ballet dancer who has to weigh in weekly at her ballet school gives her argument a whole new dimension.

Try This:

Even students who choose their topics based on a personal connection might need to brainstorm a bit about how to work it in. Should it be via a quick acknowledgement that they are a member of a community they are writing about? Or should it come in the form of a longer story, or the description of a scene they have personally witnessed?

To test the idea, look at a few different ways students in this collection have handled it. Besides the examples mentioned above, here are some other choices:

- **#60**, "Intelligence Over Diversity," is about affirmative action. Have your students read to see where this student brings in personal experience. How might it have been a different piece if the information in paragraph four was revealed in paragraph one?
- Next, have your students look at essays like "Will the Future of American Manufacturing Be Printed?" (**#64**) and "Do the Benefits of Philanthropic Companies Like Toms Outweigh the Harms?" (**#98**), in which the writers only very briefly mention themselves. Did they need to include themselves at all if they did it this way? Why or why not?

Then have students think about where in their own essays their personal stake in the topic might best be placed, and why.

➤ Tell Stories and Play on Our Feelings (Pathos)

"The best persuasive essays have a storytelling heart," writes Jay Heinrichs in his book *Thank You for Arguing*. "A story does more than entertain. It helps put the reader into cognitive ease, that most persuadable of states."[27]

Some of the essays in this collection tell a story or describe an experience that so powerfully and emotionally takes us into an argument that the rest of the evidence is secondary—the writer has already not just gotten our attention, but swayed our opinion. (And, yes, sometimes good writing blurs categories since certainly the stories Narain and Corinne tell give them authority—ethos—on those topics *and* sway our opinions via pathos.)

One of the most powerful examples of pathos *and* ethos in this collection is **#3**, Asaka Park's "I'm a Disabled Teenager, and Social Media is My Lifeline." Not only is the writing vivid and brave, but it is also a point of view many teenagers may never have considered. The way Asaka contrasts her life at school with her life online immediately gains her sympathy for her argument, but it also teaches the reader something. It is hard to argue that social media is an unalloyed negative in the lives of all teenagers after reading about what it does for Asaka.

On our webinar, Nicholas Kristof spoke to the power of stories.

"I learned this lesson when I was reporting from Darfur in 2004 and it was really frustrating because I'd make these long, dangerous and sometimes expensive trips . . . and I felt like my stories would disappear without a trace," he said.

At about the same time there were two hawks who had built a nest at the top of an expensive apartment building near Central Park -- but the building removed the nest because of all the bird droppings that resulted.

"All of New York seemed up in arms about these homeless hawks," Mr. Kristof said. "I wondered, why can't I generate the same outrage about hundreds of thousands of people being slaughtered?"

Getting people to care comes from helping them connect emotionally. Mr. Kristof points out that *after* you make that connection, you can and should bring in data and statistics to confirm your point, but that you must get your audience to feel empathy first.

People know they should care about refugees, he says, but they also have to be at work in thirty minutes and who has time? Yet if you can draw them in with the story of one refugee, you might make them care about the 60 million others fleeing crisis and conflict around the globe. That's how he came to make a video Op-Ed in 2017 about 14-year-old Elena, who was forced into a relationship with a gang member in Honduras when she was only eleven. It is called "This Is What a Refugee Looks Like."[28]

Try This:

Here are a number of good examples of the use of pathos. Which might offer relevant lessons for your students' own work?

- In "The Red Stain on Society," Holly Keaton makes us all remember the horrors of puberty to drive home her case—that talk about menstruation should be normalized and stigma-free. She opens with this disarming admission: "The first time I got my period, I had no idea what to do. I woke up with stained sheets and a feeling of humiliation in my stomach; the night before, I had, embarrassingly enough, put a pad on the wrong way" (**#46**).

- In "Under Black Cloaks," Bincheng Mao describes a scene she witnessed at a mall in Riyadh that says more than paragraphs of facts ever could (**#53**).
- A very different setting—a high school football field—is the site of Keegan Lindell's rich description of what it's like when "a man disguised as a bomb" smacks head-first into another player. He makes the reader feel the pain (**#85**).
- In "How Ableism Lives On," Hope Kurth begins with a story that can't help but make the reader experience what her brother, a 22-year-old with Down syndrome, might when he's out in public and treated like a child (**#70**).
- Students should be attentive to how their choices of nouns, verbs, and adjectives make an emotional impact. What words, phrases, or images can they use to make their readers feel their anger, experience empathy, or want to take action? Have them read Francesca Kelley's "In Nothing We Trust" (**#34**) to see how she uses emotionally potent images and loaded words to make her case: her portrayal of the world today is full of locked doors and neighbors eyeing Girl Scouts with suspicion, but a "bygone America," is a place where "neighbors relied on each other to watch the kids or borrow some sugar." Another example? The opening paragraph of "Concussion Hysteria" (**#86**), which shows how one student athlete feels about the issue.
- Another type of pathos appeal is the way many of these essays address the reader to make us see our own culpability in a problem. To observe how this technique works, your students might check out the opening paragraphs of two that force us to look at our own consumption habits: **#97**, "Shop Till You (and Humanity) Drop" and **#98**, "One-for-One Business Models: Do the Benefits of Philanthropic Companies Like Toms Outweigh the Harms?"
- Finally, even if students don't have their own tales to tell, they may have come across a story in their research that can make their argument meaningful and memorable. Eva Ferguson does a version of that when she contrasts her own ability to get treatment for her illness with the tragic story of Alec Raeshawn Smith, who died because he couldn't afford insulin (**#68**). "A Psychedelic Cure?" (**#73**) starts by

humanizing the idea of using hallucinogens as treatment for mental illness by borrowing real stories from two *New York Times* and one BBC article. And "Life Sentences for Children Should Go Away . . . For Life" (**#95**) begins with a true story about someone sentenced as a teenager to life in prison without the possibility of parole.

➤ Get Your Facts Straight and Make Sure Your Evidence Makes Your Case (Logos)

Back in 2014 when this contest began, Andrew Rosenthal, then the *Times* Opinion page editor, made a video for us[29] that reminds students of the famous quote attributed to Daniel Patrick Moynihan: "You're entitled to your own opinions. You are not entitled to your own facts."

Without strong evidence grounded in reliable facts, none of the 100 essays in this book would have made it past the first round of judging.

Amy Robinson, the English teacher in Atlanta, says she has her students look at adult-written editorials as well as the past winners of this contest to note the balance between fact and opinion. In some of the best pieces, her students were surprised to see that few sentences were statements of opinion, but that, instead, the opinions were merely implied by the facts the author chose. "They realized that the facts can lead you to a conclusion that doesn't have to be spelled out," she says.

#96 is a strong example. In "It's Time to Legalize the World's Oldest Profession" Ashlyn DesCarpentrie makes a powerful, straight-ahead argument that "Sex work is a legitimate occupation, and it's time we legalized it as such."

As she says at the end of her essay, "I am not proclaiming a moral judgment on prostitution; I am stating facts." State facts she does: She uses sources as varied as an interview with a brothel owner in Las Vegas; studies by the University of California, Australia, and the Netherlands; a quote from an HIV expert; and a Letter to the Editor in *The New York Times*. All of them serve to support statements like, "Legalizing sex work would turn it into a revenue maker."

Of course, it's not just about amassing sources and data. You also need to explain how and why your evidence speaks to your argument.

Narain Dubey, who wrote "Breaking the Blue Wall of Silence" (**#92**), says he found a mass of evidence he wanted to use, but kept asking himself, "How can I make sure everything I write is impactful to my readers?" One thing he says he learned: that statistics can be "really powerful, but also really distracting":

> *In my original piece, I probably had one or two stats for every paragraph, and at first that seemed really important, like it would really justify my argument, but then I realized it blurred the focus. In the end I focused on the stat about how black men are 3.6 times more likely to experience force by police officers as compared to whites, then I focused the whole piece around that.*

One thing I should note at this point is that we judges do not rigorously fact-check all these essays. If we did, we'd have to deliberate for four months instead of the two it already takes us. We do, however, often spot-check what we find, looking up, say, statistics that don't sound right, sources that we've never heard of, or "facts" that sound too convenient to be reliable. But it's also true that we very rarely find anything out of order. For the most part, the work of those who get to the final round is carefully constructed all the way along, and then fact-checked again before those writers finally submit.

That isn't to say, however, that some of these winners aren't guilty of lesser crimes of logic. Like professional opinion writers, these students sometimes use logical fallacies for effect—making sweeping generalizations that "everyone" does or feels or knows something, for example, or establishing a cause and effect relationship where none exists.

Because they are student writers, some faulty logic may also be inadvertent. One quick fix? Avoid making claims that overreach. In *Teaching Arguments*, Jennifer Fletcher reminds students that claims that are too broad aren't defensible, and suggests they rid their writing of "zombie words" like *always, never, everyone, no one, all, none,* etc.[30]

For an example of how to do it better, here is the opening paragraph of "The 4th R: Real Life" (**#14**), which makes a strong rhetorical case, yet uses one word—"perhaps"—to strategically soften what would otherwise have been too bold a claim:

> *Who's to blame for ballooning credit card debt and student loans? The public education system, perhaps. American high school students can recite Shakespeare's sonnets, derive advanced calculus theorems, and explain the Chinese spheres of influence. Yet these same students know little to nothing about economics and personal finance. They know of income tax only as the fifth square on the Monopoly board.*

As your students read these pieces and those of their classmates, they should get in the habit of keeping a close eye on the kinds of evidence the writers use, the sources they come from, and the logical leaps they make as a result. Spotting flaws in one's own work can make them sensitive to the ways logical fallacies are used to deliberately manipulate, in everything from advertising to politics to, yes, the work of professional opinion writers.

Try This:

- If your students have access to the full collection, let them look through a handful of essays, maybe reading just those in a section that interests them, and list the kinds of fact-based evidence they find. Quotes from experts? Statistics? Research studies? Polls? Examples? Comparisons? What else? Which make the case best? Do any detract from the point the author is making? Do any seem dubious for any reason? Why? How could the writer fix those?

  For instance, compare several pieces that argue that we need to take mental health as seriously as we take physical health. This is a topic on which we get many essays each year, and there are four good examples in this collection. Have your students look closely at how the writers of **#69**, **#72**, **#74**, and **#75** have each used statistics to make different cases about why addressing mental health is so important. To what extent do those statistics strengthen their claims?

- Students might also work with one or two essays to go through and label each sentence "fact" or "opinion" to look at the balance. Which essays do the best job of letting facts make the case so that the opinion is implied rather than stated? Which essays explain the relevance of the evidence best?

For instance, take a look at "A Change in the Menu" by Grace Silva (**#78**). How many of her statements are facts and how many opinions? How well supported do your students find her argument that we Westerners should include more bugs in our daily diets? They might contrast it with **#80**, "A Massacre of Art" that argues that pop music is an artless genre. How many of this writer's statements are opinions and how many are facts? Do you think he makes his case? Why or why not?

- How do writers whose evidence is more anecdotal than factual still use facts to bolster what they say? A good example is **#8**, "The Wonders of Wandering." Have students check out how Lucas Schroeder uses his third paragraph as a way to give backing and context to what is otherwise an argument mostly built from vivid details about his personal experience.

➤ Acknowledge Counterarguments

As we explored in the research section of this Teacher's Companion, composing a solid argument requires your students to have a full understanding of the range of perspectives on the issue so that they can take an educated, logical stance and anticipate rebuttals.

You may have to explain to them that acknowledging those counterarguments actually *strengthens* their claims, first of all because their audience may already be mentally raising these objections as they read. More importantly, airing all sides can also make a stance seem even more reasonable and trustworthy since, as Erica Lee Beaton's "listening arguments" remind us, it takes the "other side" seriously, as real people.

In essays as short as these, not every student includes a counterclaim, and even among those who do, not all truly engage it. But take a look at some who did it well.

In his essay (**#12**) about the trouble with "voluntourism," Jack Jian Kai Zhang doesn't just argue that volunteer tourism can be harmful, or that it diverts money from those who need it most, he also takes on a common counterargument—one he probably expects the reader to be thinking of by about paragraph four, which is exactly where he introduces it.

"Still," he writes, "proponents of voluntourism argue that it is better than nothing: costly, yes, but nevertheless a form of much-needed assistance to the less fortunate."

But then he deftly uses that counterargument to bring up yet *another* point to bolster his case:

> *However, this defense highlights a less obvious, and arguably more fundamental, issue with voluntourism: its roots in a colonial psyche. The notion that untrained Westerners can meaningfully better foreign communities is both unrealistic and based on an unspoken Western myth of superiority.*

Another example: In "Limiting Science Education: Limiting Ourselves" (**#20**), James Chan argues that memorization plays too big a role in high school science, and that teaching for understanding should be paramount. But he also fully considers the role of memorization by explaining its benefits and quoting an expert to make an important point about what its role should be.

As your students read, they can borrow language from all the many ways these pieces introduce their counterarguments. For instance, "some say . . ." is a classic, an easy way to nod to an opposing view without having to give details about who those "some" are or where and how they "say" it. Hope Kurth uses it well in **#70**, "How Ableism Lives On":

> *Some say that nitpicking words like "crazy" and "lame" will just start another political correctness battle, and that there is no easy way to eliminate them. But before deeming this challenge "too hard," think about how difficult it is for 48.9 million Americans to not only have a disability, but to be reminded of it in everyday conversations.*

Other writers in this collection are playful with their language as they acknowledge objections, but still engage them convincingly. In **#59**, "Good

Before God (or Any of His Religions)," Jason Barr argues that morality comes not from the divine, but from a simple need to get along in communities, and he uses animal behavior to make his point. His counterargument begins this way:

> *I can hear you now: "So what if animals are 'nice,' that doesn't make them moral." Okay, true. "Nice" is not synonymous with "moral." However . . ."*

But not every piece in this book announces its counterargument so obviously. For some, it is implied. For instance, you might have your students read **#1**, "A Generation Zer's Take on the Social Media Age," and identify the counterargument, then point to the lines where the writer is clearly referencing it.

Or, show them the way Lane Schnell's argument takes on the counterargument in its very title and first sentence? In a piece called "How 'It's Okay to Be Gay' Has Become a Lie in the Trump Era" (**#50**), Lane begins, "Straight people always seem to take delight in telling me, 'It's 2019, no one cares if you're gay or trans!'," then goes on to provide four paragraphs to show that it is "borderline dangerous to be a queer American."

Try This:

If it is difficult to convince your students that including a counterargument can make their persuasive writing stronger, an exercise from a Learning Network lesson plan[31] can make them see that they already know plenty about why and how to use them.

Pair students and let them choose from the following scenarios. Explain that to get what they want, each party needs to understand the other's position so well that they can use it to strengthen their own argument. Have them script their skit if they like or simply rehearse what they'll say. For example, they might acknowledge counterarguments by beginning, "I know what you're going to say . . ." then explaining how that line of thinking is lacking.

Scenario 1: Two friends outside a movie theater. Each wants to see a different movie.

Scenario 2: A parent and a child. The child wants a later curfew to attend a party with friends.

Scenario 3: A student and a teacher. The student wants an extension on a paper.

When students are ready, ask for several pairs to perform. After each role-play, ask the rest of the class which party had the more convincing argument and discuss why. How did the "winner" incorporate counterarguments? What effect did that have?

➤ Working in the Research: How to Quote, Paraphrase, and Transition

When do you paraphrase and when do you quote? How do you move between personal stories and research?

Luckily for your students, these 100 essays generally make these nuts-and-bolts moves with great skill. They use their quotes strategically, paraphrase the research they cite coherently and without plagiarizing, and move between paragraphs easily. Many are also adept at telling personal stories that transition seamlessly into broader "why this matters" paragraphs that put those stories into context.

Here are some ways to use them as mentors.

Try These:

A. Use quotes: sparingly and for effect.

With only 450 words to play with, these writers tend to use quotes only when someone else can say something better than they can. Sometimes that is because the person they quote brings a needed authority, and sometimes that's because the quotes themselves are especially apt or elegant. Many use them in their last paragraphs to make a bigger point.

For example:

- In "Why We Should Teach the Truth About American History" (**#18**), Patrick Wang ends his essay by quoting a Yale professor as a way to put into historical context his whole argument about how issues like slavery should be taught:

> *By indoctrinating students with the idea of "American exceptionalism" rather than teaching them the truth about American history, the only people we end up fooling are ourselves. As the Yale professor of American Studies Jon Butler puts it, "America emerged out of many contentious issues. If we understand those issues, [only then can we] figure out how to move forward in the present." Thus, knowing the truth about American history should not be a privilege. It is a right.*

What other essays in this collection use a quote in the last paragraph? Which are especially effective?

B. Paraphrase to summarize dense material in a way that furthers your argument.

You can find examples of excellent paraphrasing all over this collection, but this essay may be one that is especially interesting to students since it takes on a topic they will all likely be familiar with.

- In "Vice for Vice" (**#71**), 15-year-old Eugene Hong argues about vaping that "In order to truly lessen drug use, government and schools have to go after image, not just drugs themselves." In this paragraph, his second, he summarizes the history of the relationship between nicotine addiction and image, using a 1997 *Times* article, "Joe Camel, a Giant in Tobacco Marketing, Is Dead at 23," as his source for some of the information, and "Teenagers Embrace JUUL, Saying It's Discreet Enough To Vape In Class," a 2017 NPR piece, as another.

  Students might note not only how he paraphrases these pieces, but also how he uses a telling quote from the NPR piece, which emphasizes a point he makes earlier—that the "cat and mouse game" between teachers and students around vaping only adds to its allure.

> *Joe Camel, the icon of tobacco conglomerate R. J. Reynolds, was executed in 1997, after nearly a decade of representing the Camel brand of cigarettes. The reasoning behind the federal government's decision to outlaw the swaggering camel was that he made smoking seem carefree and enticing to youth.*

> *Currently we are experiencing a more subtle version of the Joe Camel, in which vape pens such as Juul are reclaiming fun, risqué smoking. Not only do vapers have a nearly endless array of flavors to choose from, they also have apparatus that can disappear in a closed fist, according to a review of the Juul pen by NPR, which says owning a Juul is like a badge of honor. "Y'all this kid came into my 7th period to get a juul and we all started laughing when he left so the teacher was really confused," according to @hyphyybriannaa, quoted in the study.*

(Note: Our contest demands that students list at least two sources—one from the *Times* and one from outside the *Times*. Some students report just those, but others, like this writer, list all the sources they use. We also do not specify that students must footnote, though many use MLA style and put those references right into the text itself as well.)

C. Try transitioning into research by using this simple technique. Many of our student winners open their piece with an engaging, often personal, first paragraph, a hook to get us reading, then move into the research that supports or explains their point of view. Here are some examples so your students can try it, too:

In "We Need Music in Our Schools" (**#29**), Gabe M. tells us about his own experience first, but his second paragraph begins "Research shows that music education boosts students' academic success." He goes on to detail how, quoting everyone from the U.S. Dept of Education to Pythagoras. His third paragraph then uses another elegant transition to deepen his case. It begins: "But music's benefits extend beyond school."

Abigail Hogan does the same in "Discourse Is Democracy: Allowing Uncensored Speech on College Campuses" (**#43**). Her first paragraph pulls us in, and her second piles up statistics to show why her opening paragraph matters.

Emma Chiu begins her piece on self-driving cars (**#65**) with a nod to that "teenage rite of passage: learning to drive," then moves immediately into her research on how our driving habits are changing.

And in her essay about CBD in consumer products (**#99**), Emily Milgrim opens with a story about how close her toddler cousins came to accidentally drinking seltzer infused with CBD, then uses it to show how ubiquitous CBD is becoming—and why that is a problem.

➤ Issue a Call to Action or Suggest a Solution

The guidelines for our contest ask that students do this as part of the 450-word package. Why? Because reading an editorial that simply lays out a problem feels unsatisfying and incomplete. Why bring a problem up if there's nothing that can be done about it?

The section of this book where our teen writers do that most concretely is the chapter on school, and it's easy to understand why. Students are experts—at sitting all day (**#21**), at being bullied in gym class (15), at lockdown drills (17), at standardized testing (16), and at the endless stress around getting perfect grades to get into a perfect college (28). The calls to action in this section are particularly passionate and especially specific. Many suggest changes to the curriculum, whether to make science more interesting (20), to "tell the truth about American history" (18), or to add courses in financial literacy (14).

If you're looking beyond the chapter on school, Lila McNamee's piece, **#35**, is a good one to consider. She says she knew what she wanted to write about right away: the one-child policy in China. Adopted from China as a baby herself, she was emotionally invested in the subject and came to it with many questions, but didn't know exactly what she wanted to see change—until she began researching.

Lila watched a video, "Somewhere Between,"[32] about adopted girls from China, and in it one finds her birth parents. That made her realize that in the United States, especially with the advent of sites like 23andMe, adopted children are often able to trace their original families, but in China it is very rare because the government keeps those records closed.

Her call to action?

> *Although I take Mandarin and feel connected to Chinese culture, I wish I knew more about me. What is my family medical history? Do I have siblings? Who do I look like?*

The Chinese government took these things from me and 175,000 others. It's time they try to make amends. I don't want a generic letter saying, "We're sorry." I want a letter with my genetic information. The government could set up a program where families could submit their DNA, the approximate birth date of their child, and their province/district, giving Chinese adoptees a real chance to find the parents that were forced to give them away. I dream of meeting my biological family, and I think the Chinese government owes me the opportunity to make that happen.

Try This:

Not all the essays in this collection do an excellent job at every element we identify on our rubric, of course. We judge them holistically, and sometimes an essay makes the cut even if an individual element is weak.

If your students have the full collection, ask them: Are there essays in this collection without real calls to action or solutions? If the writers could add an additional paragraph, what might you suggest they do to make that aspect of the piece stronger? Why?

Or, use some of the essays that have successfully incoporated this element as mentor texts:

- Many of the calls to action in these essays are quite small and personal and written directly to fellow teenagers. For example, Lola Byers-Ogle suggests that we stop using language about mental illness casually or jokingly (**#69**). In **#74**, "We Are the Generation of Self-Deprecation," Faith Christiansen ends with this paragraph designed to help Gen Z know "it's okay to love yourself":

  Use all of your quirks to define your success. Pay attention to how many times you put yourself down and stop doing it. Replace every negative thought with a compliment and become an advocate for self-love and self-worth.

- A simple "I propose" to begin the final paragraph can both suggest a call to action and take your argument further. Check out how Charlie Gstalder does this in "The Future of the #MeToo Movement Through the Eyes of a 17-Year-Old Boy" (**#49**).

➤ "Layering in the Brush Strokes": Play with Voice, Word Choice, and Tone

If there's one quality of the thousands of essays we get each spring that immediately signals to us judges that we're in the hands of a good writer, it's evidence that a student is having fun with language. Even the most serious topic can have tone-appropriate flourishes—what Kabby Hong, borrowing an idea from the author and teacher Harry Noden,[33] calls "brush strokes."

He uses the work of previous contest winners to show his students how playing with syntax and vocabulary, adding similes and metaphors, using repetition and rhetorical questions, can all make writing sparkle.

"Trying to teach voice and personality—that's so hard," he says. "But with this contest it's easy, because you really honor and respect funky headlines, interesting uses of dashes and colons and great, weird first lines. All the writing has life and vibrant energy. When the kids see that, they're like, okay, I get why voice matters—and not just because it's part of the rubric."

Indeed, Anushka Agarwal, the author of "Civil Obedience" (**#31**), says that she felt writing her essay was such good practice with voice that it informed her college applications. "I literally had my editorial contest essay open in a tab for inspiration as I was writing my college essay," she says. "Writing this editorial made it so much easier, because the format is actually fairly similar: Who I am as a person, but grounded in facts."

Susan Rothbard, Anushka's teacher at her suburban New Jersey high school, shares some of the credit for Anushka's winning essay since before the class wrote their own, she had them analyze examples from both students and adults.

"We put examples up on a screen and looked at the strategies past winners of the contest used, as well as strategies people like [*Times* Op-Ed columnists] Gail Collins and Frank Bruni use. It shows my students how to write about important issues that are current in the world, but how to do it with voice, not just by giving information," she says.

Among others, Mr. Hong's students look at the careful diction in the opening to "In Three and a Half Hours, an Alarm Will Go Off" (**#13**), including the choice of verbs in the first sentence ("drag," "plop," "dive") that show how harried and stressed the authors are, as well as the sarcastic use of "luxurious" to describe five hours of sleep. These descriptive opening sentences are followed by four short, declarative sentences to bring home the writers' contention that this is just how life is for high school juniors:

> *In three and a half hours, an alarm will go off, and one of the authors of this article will drag himself out of bed, plop his head in a bowl of cereal, and dive into a swimming pool. The other has a luxurious five hours to look forward to, but don't worry, he'll pay for it tomorrow night; that science fair project won't finish itself, after all.*
>
> *We are both in high school. We are both juniors. And we both have yet to go to bed.*
>
> *Welcome to a normal Monday morning.*

When you read an essay like this, you can hear the writers' natural voices, much as if you were having a conversation with them, but you also have a sense that their language has been deliberately kicked up a notch. Which is exactly what many of the essay winners I interviewed recommended.

Nora Fellas, who wrote **#33**, "Lessons for 2020 Democratic Presidential Candidates, From a Soon-to-be First-Time Voter," and whose "before" and "after" versions you can read in full in Appendix B, is especially sensitive to how to change her language and register for different audiences. As she reveals in her essay, she runs an Instagram account with over 100,000 followers, and there, she says, she writes exactly as she speaks. She is also on her school newspaper's staff, so she understands the difference between journalistic writing and academic essays. She positions this contest somewhere between the "more formal and formulaic" essays she writes in school and the very informal posts on her Instagram. "For this contest it seemed like it was okay to have a spoken kind of style. It's important to be authentic, and to make sure it flows."

Nora went through her piece to replace certain words and phrases with better ones, but she shares a warning all our judges would agree with: don't just go through and replace everyday words with bigger ones. "You can tell when a person is using a thesaurus too much," Nora says. "There will be that one word that doesn't flow with the rest of the sentence."

The piece with the most obvious word play is **#76**, "Shakespeare: Friend, Not Foe." Angela Chen grounds her argument in Shakespearean language to make her case. When I interviewed her, I could see that wordplay came naturally. It's clear how much fun she has choosing words, making images, and fiddling with tone even when she's just giving advice to other students. Here is what she suggests:

> *Care about what you're arguing for. If it doesn't get you lively, seething, full of love, then it might be more difficult to write well about . . . Make your voice fresh. People don't want to hear the same phrasing of the same argument that has been in circulation around the internet for years. Pick a topic that makes people go either "Oh, wow," or "You did NOT just say that." Attack it in fresh, combative ways. Play around with the wording. Mess up the sentence structure. Be a linguistic cook.*

Try This:

- Have your students take a look at **#51**, "You Don't Need to Glitter Things Pink to Get Me into STEM," to note all the ways Abby W. mocks the marketers who have reached out to her, a girl interested in the sciences, by "feminizing" their pitches. Have them underline all the words and phrases she uses that play on this theme.
- Or invite them to trace the way Bridget Smith uses a Thanksgiving metaphor throughout **#30**, "Dinner Table Politics," beginning and ending with it, and briefly referencing it in the body paragraphs. How does using that metaphor as a frame strengthen her message?
- There's no better essay for showing how effective specific, sensory details can be than "The Wonders of Wandering" (**#8**). Imagine if, instead of "rode a stubborn horse named Prince with a rodeo stuntman in Wyoming," Lucas Schroeder had simply written "rode horses

in Wyoming"? Your students might identify the places where those descriptions sing, then find sentences in their own work where detail can make a difference.

- Repetition is such an effective rhetorical technique that your students probably already realize they can find it in everything from "I Have a Dream" to "Annabel Lee." But take a look at how Marco Alvarez, in "Indigenous: Unheard, But Loud" (**#58**), uses it in the last paragraph of his essay to describe what "the casual American" won't know, and how he ratchets up the stakes with each repetition. Or check out how Holly Keaton uses "because" over and over in the final paragraph of "The Red Stain on Society" (**#46**). Where might your students use repetition in their own work to make a point?
- Or what about the "brushstrokes" in "It's Time for America to Start Feeling the Love for Ultimate Frisbee" (**#89**)? Have your students note the playful language, from the way Alex Kucich describes the sport's hippie origins to funny bits of wordplay like, "Why, then, is Disc dissed?"

Then as they finish their own essays and start to edit, you might have them consciously layer in their own "brush strokes" by answering questions like:

- What clichés have you used and what can you say instead?
- Where have you used a general noun or verb where a specific one might work better?
- Where have you repeated words—not for effect, but for lack of imagination? What can you substitute?
- Where have you told readers something when showing it, through an image, story, quote, or analogy, might make it more vivid?
- How varied are your sentences? Try reading the piece aloud and listening to their rhythm.
- What punctuation have you used, and how does it affect the way each sentence reads?
- What stylistic flourishes do you admire in the essays in this collection? Are there any you might want to borrow for your own work?

- Finally, ask yourself, does this writing sound like me? Read your piece out loud again and listen to the voice and rhythm. You might also ask your friends to read it and point out what words and phrases sound the most like your natural voice.

➤ Make Your Conclusion Memorable

Like wasting the first few lines of an essay, squandering the last can tell a reader a great deal about how in control and invested a writer is. A lazy "In conclusion . . ." that just barely rewrites the original thesis statement is dull to read and, more important, doesn't offer the audience anything new to think about.

One of the most powerful conclusions in this collection can be found in Daina Kalnina's essay, **#17**. Written in 2017, before the Parkland shootings put the topic on everyone's radar, Daina was already arguing that the lockdown drills at most schools left students dangerously vulnerable.

In "Stopping Bullets with Locked Doors and Silence Is Already Pulling the Trigger," she makes her case in three dense opening paragraphs that describe the drill her school uses and advocate for an alternative. Then, she brings the essay to a close with two short paragraphs, each a sentence long:

> *It's unnerving that the students of this country must learn how to cope with active shooters.*
>
> *It's even more unnerving that current procedures say that they should sit, wait and die.*

Ask your students: What is the effect of ending that way, especially on that final word?

Nora Fellas, whose complete "before" and "after" essays can be found in Appendix B, made a lot of edits to bring a 743-word piece down to the required 450 words, but the revision she made to her conclusion is perhaps the most effective. Here is how it read originally:

> *To the 2020 candidates: The key to earning my vote, and the votes of my peers is not showing us how "cool" you are by using slang. We don't want to see that you can take the advice of your millennial intern, we want to see that your original ideas reflect the issues that affect us, like gun control and climate change—otherwise, we will just stay home.*

Nora credits her teacher, Ellen Cowhey, with pointing out that the original essay "ends on a sad note," and suggesting that, instead, she finish with a "positive call to action."

Here is how the editorial now reads:

> *To the 2020 candidates: the key to earning our vote isn't pandering to us. Rather, we want to see that you genuinely care about the issues that matter to us. If you do that, you won't need to worry about spreading your message on Instagram. We'll do it for you.*

There are many fewer examples of great endings in this collection than there are great beginnings, but here are some more to consider.

- The clever way Isabel Hwang alludes to and subverts the Marie Kondo "Life-Changing Magic of Tidying Up" phenomenon in the title and the conclusion of her "Life-Changing Magic of Being Messy" (**#9**).
- The story that ends Safa Saleh's "America First" (**#40**).
- The satisfying and clever way both "The Real Solution" (**#45**) and "Let Children of Color Be Characters, Too" (**#79**) use the technique of calling back a detail from the first paragraph in their final paragraph.
- How an essay about the joys of literature, "To Read or Not to Read?" (**#83**), both begins and ends with a quotation from a famous author (and, of course, the title itself is a nod to a famous literary quotation).

Try This:

Challenge your students to write a terrible conclusion on purpose. Sometimes trying to break the rules can teach you how to follow them, and in my experience it also sensitizes students to everything from grammar errors to clichés. If nothing else, it breaks the tension and loosens students' thinking up.

To do it, students can work with their individual topics, or they can all experiment with the same general topic. Or give them all the same last paragraph from an essay in this collection and challenge them to make it as boring, meaningless, and repetitive as possible. Then invite them to read their work aloud and battle to see whose will be crowned "worst."

➤ Edit It Down to the Essentials

New Jersey humanities teacher Sarah Gross says she often works with newspaper Op-Eds precisely because they are so concise.

"Concision is what my kids struggle with the most," she says. "It's almost like they have imposter syndrome, so they think anything they hand in has to sound super, super smart, but instead it's sometimes just eight pages of nonsense."

When I interviewed her, she had just finished working with her students to get their editorials down to 450 words—though at the moment one of them had a thesis statement that, alone, was 64 words long.

Ms. Gross says the benefit of writing a short essay is that it "actually forces them to go through revision. I think they skip that step—kind of fake it—elsewhere in school. For this contest, they have to revise. No one just naturally writes 450 words when they're making a strong argument, so this assignment makes them trim, and encourages them to have other eyes on it to help them do that."

Whatever your students are writing, it can be a revelation for them to see where they repeat ideas rather than moving an argument forward. Amanda Lentino suggests taking a highlighter and showing them how many words they waste. "I tell them, 'You're not proving anything yet.' I highlight every single claim that's just reworded differently and in the end there are some papers where 80 percent is highlighted."

Try This:

To introduce the notion of the 450-word editorial, you could do no better than turning to Eric Vogt's wry essay, "Cutting it Short" (**#25**).

One of our 2014 finalists, his piece uses the contest requirement itself to talk about his realization that school only teaches kids to write lengthy pieces—and, in our text-message world, learning to write short should "knock the traditional essay from its long-held dominance." But he also notes that, although writing a short piece may initially seem easy, something you could quickly whip up the night before it's due, it is actually far more difficult, an "art for which current high school students are not prepared." Do your students agree?

You might also put them in pairs and invite them to do for each other what Ms. Lentino does for her students: Read each other's work and highlight where it is repetitious.

➤ Don't Waste Your Headline

If your students are using the full collection, invite them to flip through and list which headlines jump out. Perhaps:

"To Bae or Not To Bae"
"Am I Dangerous?"
"Egghead Son vs. Airhead Daughter?"
"Shop Till You (And Humanity) Drop"
"A Prodigy for Your Progeny"
"There Is No Happily Ever After Without Once Upon a Time"

What qualities make the ones they liked particularly provocative or interesting to them? Why? Which headlines could be stronger? How?

For some students, the headline will be the first thing they think of. For most, it will be among the last. Either way, remind them not to waste it—especially if, as for our contest, there are length limits that mean every word must count.

Ask them: How can your title do some work for you? Can it announce your subject, but in a catchy way? Can it pick up on language in the piece itself somehow? Can it state something surprising or counterintuitive? Can it be the "bumper sticker" argument Nicholas Kristof talks about? Can it say something controversial that you know readers will want to argue?

Try This:

Have students experiment with writing at least three possible headlines to test out on others. They might try:

- Writing in the form of a question ("Is It Actually Smart to Sit Still?"; "Am I Dangerous?")
- Using a provocative or quirky detail or description from their essay that they know will get attention or make people wonder ("The Unspoken Alphabet Problem"; "Inmates Aren't Animals"; "A Change in the Menu"; "Why We Stayed Up Until Midnight Finishing This Editorial").
- Borrowing from the structure of a headline in this collection—though please don't use "Why I, a Heterosexual Teenage Boy . . ." since we already get so many of those. (Maybe instead "Why We Must _________" or "The Trouble With _________" or "It's Time for _________".)

➤ Get Feedback

A secret that few teenagers know is that nearly every piece of writing that gets published in the real world first gets edited.

The essays they read on newspaper opinion pages have been improved, sometimes significantly, by the invisible labor of someone behind the scenes. A novel goes through draft after draft after draft, with readers, editors, proofreaders, and copy editors along the way. Even this short book has been through many rounds of readers and editing, and the student essays themselves all went through a light copy edit for grammar, punctuation, and spelling even *after* they won.

"Every writer needs an editor," says former *Times* Opinion page editor Andrew Rosenthal on the video he made for our site. "After you've written your editorial, give it to someone you trust to read, and listen to what they say. If they don't understand it, that means it's probably not clear."[34]

One pleasant surprise for me as a former English teacher who often assigned it: every single student I interviewed who wrote their essay in a classroom setting mentioned, without prompting, how valuable peer editing was in helping them figure out what to say and how to say it.

In fact, English teacher Shari Krapels, who helped Asaka Park with her essay, says that one of the reasons she thinks Asaka felt comfortable composing such a personal and revealing piece (#3), is because her class regularly shares their work with each other, and "since all the kids in the room had seen it and liked it, it wasn't a huge emotional leap to send it in."

Bridget Smith, author of "Dinner Table Politics" (#30), raises another reason for a teacher to make sure students hear each other's work.

"My teacher would ask permission first, but then she would read aloud people's paragraphs, and you'd get to hear from kids you don't usually hear from in class. There were all these really interesting perspectives from quiet students," she says.

Try This:

In peer groups, you might return to some of ideas listed under the first section of this book, Reading Like Writers, but this time, have students apply them to each other's work instead of to the essays in this collection. For instance, what could they learn by trading essays to annotate for structure?

V. Finding Authentic Audiences: Getting Student Work Out Into the World

When students send their work out into the world, it changes everything—at least according to the many teachers who answered a call on The Learning Network to tell us why they encourage it.[35]

Having an authentic audience lets young people see that their voices and ideas are valuable, they say. It proves they can do something real with what they've learned. And the work itself gets better: students are more engaged, more thoughtful about their choices, and more eager to revise. Perhaps most important, they begin to think of themselves as real writers, not just students who produce papers for a grade.

Kabby Hong makes the point that schools celebrate when their sports teams win championships, but there is rarely a "corresponding hyping up of academic achievement." Sending work out elevates writing to that level. When his students win a contest or get published somewhere, he takes a photo of the student and the work and frames it, and he also sends word to his town's press association. "They become local celebrities for awhile," he says.

In fact, it is common for kids who win one of our contests to be honored by their local papers. The first year we ran a podcast contest, for instance, the *Chicago Post-Tribune* wrote about the three boys from Gary, Indiana, who produced a lively piece that interviewed experts about their hometown. "Gary teens picked for *New York Times* podcast contest have 'the willingness to be bold and ask questions,'" read the headline of the piece, which also featured a photo of the students.[36]

And if you need yet another reason to send student work out, consider this: for many high school students, the first time they'll write in their own natural voices for an adult audience they've never met is for their college admissions essays. That's a pretty high-stakes rhetorical situation to face with no practice.

My own twins are cases in point. They went to two different high schools, both of which prized writing across the curriculum and gave them rigorous practice in composing things like research papers, lab reports, and literary essays. Neither of my kids, however, was involved in the kinds of extracurriculars like a school newspaper that could have given them regular opportunities to write for people outside the classroom—and none of their in-class assignments made up that gap. Even though I had been an English teacher myself for 10 years, and a literacy coach for 9 (not to mention, of course, editor of a *Times* website that is centered on "student voice"), it wasn't until I watched them struggle through draft after draft that I realized how often that "authentic audience" component is missing in school, and how useful it would be to include. Just for starters, if it had been more natural to them to think first about the audience they were trying to persuade, they might have immediately considered which topics have become college admissions clichés and avoided them. They might also have been used to wrestling with register, and therefore more comfortable writing in their real voices from the beginning, rather than moving from excessively formal first drafts to pieces that, eventually, sounded just like them.

So if your students have used the advice in this book to write better opinion pieces, make sure they leave your classroom somehow. Here are a few ways to do that.

➤ Help Students Think Broadly about the Right Audiences for Their Messages

What are your students writing about? Who needs to hear it? How can they reach those people?

Let your students think about these questions in relation to their own work, and choose individually what they'd like to send out and where it should go. What communities might be most interested in their message? Who are the stakeholders? Where can they find them? How can they craft their message to best appeal to them?

They might start small, with opportunities in their school and local area. For instance, the school newspaper or website could be a home for some of this work, as could a local newspaper, radio station, or library.

Finding the right fit might require some research. For instance, let's say a student has read that some colleges offer "happiness" classes that teach stressed-out students how to have more satisfying lives[37]. She's inspired: this kind of positive psychology approach, which encourages healthy behavioral changes, can help secondary students too, she thinks—and she knows first-hand the toll bad habits can take on teenagers' mental and physical health. So she writes a piece arguing that high schools must implement such a course. This essay has a natural audience in the form of her fellow students and her school's faculty and administration, so publishing it in the school newspaper makes sense. But she might also think bigger, perhaps getting her work to the school board or to district-level administrators, which might require turning her essay into a letter, or even a short speech. She might also reach out to local organizations or institutions that focus on teenage health, to some of the colleges that offer such a course, or to related national organizations she's come across in her research. All of these places might have good advice for getting her message out, even if they don't offer publication opportunities. And, of course, she could find online organizations or sites devoted to voices on this issue, related social media–based conversations or campaigns to participate in, or, of course, writing contests like ours.

Any of these opportunities would offer this student authentic practice with questions of audience and purpose, and with the choices of language and tone that naturally follow. And it has been my experience—as a teacher, a school-newspaper advisor, an editor, and a mother—that when young people have urgent things to say and they approach adult gatekeepers with good ideas for ways to get their message out there, they are, more often than not, enthusiastically received.

Try This:

Make sending work out a requirement—but flood your students with options.

Every semester, students in Christa Forster's Houston English class have to send out at least one piece of writing. What and where is up to them; simply doing it earns the grade. Over the years, many have been surprised by winning Scholastic Art & Writing awards, getting published in the local paper, or being honored in Learning Network contests. Ms. Forster says it is a remarkably effective way to make students feel "seen." It also changes the classroom dynamic: You are no longer the sole judge of their work, but, instead, a coach to a community of writers.

She keeps an extensive list of places to submit and says matching the student and genre to the appropriate opportunity is also a great way to differentiate and help individual kids make progress in the moment. And she does something even more powerful: she models the process herself. Ms. Forster, a writer of poetry, fiction and essays, shows her students the progress of her own submissions to journals and contests by sharing with them a list of what's been accepted and rejected, one she maintains via the online platform submittable.com. She explains:

I want my students to understand that we must be willing to be vulnerable if we want to succeed. I wish one of my teachers had taught me how to handle getting rejections when I was younger. I tell the students, "I want you to get used to failure. That's why I require you to submit your work. If your work gets published, or wins a prize, then kudos! But even more kudos to you if your work gets rejected—and you don't give up.

➤ Be Prepared for Publication to Change Lives

Since we judge our Student Editorial Contest blind and, until we've chosen our winners, have no idea of the names, genders, schools, or ages of any of the students, it's been a nice surprise to hear from several teachers that the kids who win are often not the ones everyone *expects* to win. Kabby Hong's theory? That high-achieving students are often so good at the "game of school" that they don't take the same creative risks as kids who feel they have less on the line.

"You tend to pick kids who are not the prototypical 4.0 perfect kids, at least the ones who've placed from my school. That's pretty cool to see, because my students think this one kid will always get an A, and often students from left field do better. That flips the script: Sally was supposed to win but she didn't," Mr. Hong says.

He mentions two students, in particular, who, he says, have had their lives changed by being chosen as honorable mentions. (Since we chose from only winners and runners up for this collection, however, neither of those essays has been reprinted here.)

"One wrote about her biracial identity. She'd been struggling in my class, but after she got that acknowledgement, she had so much confidence. It was really remarkable how she started to own her space once she got a stamp of approval from that respected source, *The New York Times*," he says.

Another student has an even more dramatic story: He came out to the school and his classmates as transgender and gay in his essay, which was about searching for books that portrayed people like him.

"I think great writing is about emotional risk, and this student risked everything," says Mr. Hong. "I don't know if my AP Language and Composition class was a very happy place for him at the beginning—he was very,

very quiet and had a hard time engaging—but when he wrote that essay, it all came together. It was the perfect marriage of writer and topic. I was so proud of him."

For some students, validation outside school or home is something they desperately need. In a piece on our site, Arizona English teacher Andrea Avery explained it this way:

> *Students seem to feel legitimized as writers. When their work is acknowledged by a contest or publication—if they "win"—they get their first sense that their work is being considered on its own merits. They are skeptical about their parents' (often effusive, unwavering) praise and they are scarred by their parents' (often hypercritical) judgment. They also are so aware that they are, in their English teachers' minds, associated with a grade. They think a "B-in-English-kid" will never be seen as the best poet. So when they are "judged" by someone who doesn't already love them—or condemn them—unconditionally, they take that judgment a different kind of seriously."*[37]

I asked all the students I spoke to how winning our contest affected them. Every single one used the word "confidence."

Noah Spencer, who wrote the "Why I, a Heterosexual Teenage Boy" essay referenced many times in this Teacher's Companion, says, "I was really excited and proud, and still to this day if I had to pick an accomplishment I'd say that's the biggest one. The program I went to for university had a lot of very strong writers, and at times I felt a lack of confidence, but when I'd get really down I'd think of my essay and remember I could do it."

Try This:

We hope that you'll use this book as inspiration to send your students to our contest, which, as far as we know, will be held every school year from now until The Learning Network ceases to exist.

The real goal of this book, of course, is to empower students to find their *own* audiences and purposes, for whatever it is they most want to say.

What will your students write? Who will they write it for? And how can you help make sure they are heard?

500 Prompts for Argument Writing

The questions below are all drawn from The New York Times Learning Network's Student Opinion feature, which has published a fresh question every school day since 2009.

Online, each day's piece links to and excerpts a related Times article for context, and all are open to comment from teenagers around the world.

TECHNOLOGY AND LIFE ONLINE

Does technology make us more alone?

Is social media making us more narcissistic?

What social media account would you consider deleting?

Should what you say on social media be grounds for getting fired?

Would you be willing to pay for Facebook or Google in exchange for your privacy?

Are anonymous social media networks dangerous?

Should people be allowed to obscure their identities online?

Is our culture of online shaming out of control?

Are digital photographs too plentiful to be meaningful?

Do you worry we are filming too much?

Should children be social media influencers?

Would you want to create content for social media as a full-time lifestyle?

Does grammar still matter in the age of Twitter?

Should tech giants be in the business of teaching children how to be good digital citizens?

Are you the same person on social media as you are in real life?

Is the love of our phones hurting our relationships?

Is the language of texting, gifs, and emojis changing our communication for the better?

What are the five greatest inventions of all time?

Are the web filters at your school too restrictive?

Does technology in the classroom ever get in the way of learning?

When should cellphones be educational tools?

Should there be more educational video games in school?

Is online learning as good as face-to-face learning?

How would you feel about a computer grading your essays?

Do machines represent a threat to humans?

Are self-driving vehicles the wave of the future?

Do you think recreational drones are safe?

What role will robots play in our future?

Do you worry about your digital privacy?

Should facial recognition technology be banned?

Do you believe in any online conspiracy theories?

How do you know if what you read online is true?

Should Facebook fact-check political speech?

Can social media be a tool for learning and growth in schools?

What rules, if any, should there be about phone use during live performances?

Do memes make the world a better place?

TEENAGE LIFE AND GEN Z

When should you be able to buy cigarettes, drink alcohol, vote, drive, and fight in wars?

When you are old enough to vote, will you?

What can older people learn from your generation?

Does your generation have too much self-esteem?

Is your generation more self-centered than earlier generations?

Do "shame and blame" work to change teenage behavior?

Do you think teenagers can make a difference in the world?

Is teenage "voluntourism" wrong?

Is prom worth it?

Are there activities you used to love that are now so competitive they aren't fun anymore?

Does your generation experience more anxiety than other generations?

What do older generations misunderstand about teenagers today?

Have you ever taken a stand that isolated you from your peers?

Is it important for teenagers to participate in political activism?

Do you think porn influences the way teenagers think about sex?

Should you always have the right to wear what you want?

How much does your neighborhood define who you are?

What current teen trends annoy you? Why?

When do pranks cross the line to become bullying?

What words or phrases do you think are overused?

GENDER

Do parents have different hopes and standards for sons than for daughters?

Is school designed more for girls than boys?

Is single-sex education still useful?

Is there too much pressure on girls to have "perfect" bodies?

How much pressure do boys face to have the perfect body?

What does it mean to be "a real man"?

Do we need to teach boys and men to be more emotionally honest?

Is it okay for men and boys to comment on women and girls on the street?

What should we do to fight sexual violence against young women?

Why aren't there more girls in leadership roles?

Why aren't more girls choosing to pursue careers in math, science, and technology?

Now that women can serve in all combat roles in the U.S. military, should they also be required to register for the draft?

Do female athletes get short shrift?

Is it harder being a girl?

Do we need new ways to identify gender and sexuality?

Should toys be more gender-neutral?

Should transgender people be allowed to use the bathroom of their choice?

What rules should apply to transgender athletes when they compete?

Is it okay to refuse to serve same-sex couples based on religious beliefs?

Are women better at compromising and collaborating?

Do boys have less intense friendships than girls?

Do we need more female superheroes?

What messages about gender have you gotten from music?

Do you feel constricted by gender norms?

Do you consider yourself a feminist?

DATING AND SEX

Should couples live together before marriage?

Is dating a thing of the past?

Is hookup culture leaving your generation unhappy and unprepared for love?

How should children be taught about puberty and sex?

Are affirmative consent rules a good idea?

Should birth control pills be available to teenage girls without a prescription?

Should the morning-after pill be sold over the counter to people under 17?

How should educators and legislators deal with minors who "sext"?

How should parents address internet pornography?

Do you think porn influences the way teenagers think about sex?

What constitutes sexual consent?

Should your significant other be your best friend?

How big a problem is teen "sexting"?

RACE, ETHNICITY, AND DIVERSITY

Why is race so hard to talk about?

Is America backsliding on race?

Is fear of "the other" poisoning public life?

How much racism do you face in your daily life?

Is your generation really "postracial"?

How should parents teach their children about race and racism?

How should schools address race and racism?

Does your school seem integrated?

Do you ever talk about issues of race and class with your friends?

Does the United States owe reparations to the descendants of enslaved people?

Is it offensive for sports teams to use Native American names and mascots?

Do we need more diverse superheroes?

Is Hollywood becoming more diverse?

Should schools strive for racial diversity among teachers?

Do you support affirmative action in college admissions?

SPORTS

Are some youth sports too intense?

Should there be stricter rules about how coaches treat their players?

Should high schools drop football because too many players are getting injured?

If football is so dangerous to players, should we be watching it?

Is cheerleading a sport?

Has baseball lost its cool?

What new sport should the Olympics add?

Do sports teams have a responsibility to hold players to a standard of personal conduct?

Should athletes who dope have to forfeit their titles and medals?

Should women's basketball lower the rims?

Do fans put too much pressure on their favorite professional athletes?

How much should fans be allowed to distract opposing teams?

Does a championship game always need to have a winner (and a loser)?

Are some extreme sports too extreme?

How young is too young to climb Mount Everest?

Should colleges fund wellness programs instead of sports?

Where should colleges and sports teams draw the line in selling naming rights?

Should college athletes be paid?

What is your reaction to the NFL's rules about players kneeling for the National Anthem?

What are your thoughts on sports betting?

Should technology in sports be limited?

Does better sports equipment unfairly improve athletic ability?

How would you change your favorite sport?

Who is the G.O.A.T. (Greatest of All Time)?

What sport needs a rule change?

What game should be redesigned?

Should male and female athletes be paid the same?

Are advanced statistics helping or hurting sports?

Should blowouts be allowed in youth sports?

How should we punish sports cheaters?

THE ARTS AND ENTERTAINMENT

Can you separate art from the artist?

Should art come with trigger warnings?

What artists do you consider "sellouts"? Why?

Do we need art in our lives?

Should art that makes people mad be removed?

Should society support artists and others pursuing creative works?

Should displays of art be welcome in all public spaces?

Does pop culture deserve serious academic study?

How much does an artist's personal beliefs influence your opinion of their work?

Is the digital era improving or ruining the experience of art?

Can creativity be scheduled?

What movies, shows, or books need sequels, spin-offs, or new episodes?

Does reality TV promote dangerous stereotypes and behaviors?

Does TV capture the diversity of America yet?

What makes a good TV show finale?

Why do we like reality shows so much?

Should children be allowed to compete on TV?

What stereotypical characters make you cringe?

Why do we like to watch rich people on TV and in the movies?

Does live theater offer something you just can't get watching movies or TV?

What—if anything—does the current Hollywood film industry lack?

Do you think child stars have it rough?

What makes a good commercial?

Should stores sell violent video games to minors?

Do violent video games make people more violent in real life?

Should you feel guilty for killing zombies?

Can a video game be a work of art?

What game would you like to redesign?

How sexist is the gaming world?

Are awards shows worth watching anymore?

What stereotypical pop-culture characters make you cringe?

What current musicians do you think will stand the test of time?

What musician, actor, or author should be a superstar but hasn't quite made it yet?

How much can an artist borrow from earlier musicians before it becomes stealing?

Who does hip-hop belong to?

What can you predict about the future of the music industry?

Will musical training make you more successful?

What messages about gender have you gotten from music?

Are comic book movies ruining film?

Are paper books better than ebooks?

Does reading a book count more than listening to one?

To what writer would you award a prize?

Are shortened versions of classic adult literature right for young children?

Do you prefer your children's book characters obedient or contrary?

Do we still need libraries?

Has a novel ever helped you understand yourself or your world better?

How much power do books have to teach young people tolerance of others?

What books do you think every teenager should read?

Who are the characters that authors should be writing about?

Are there books that should be banned from your school library?

Is there any benefit to reading books you hate?

Should graffiti be protected?

Are there topics that should be off limits to comedy?

PARENTING AND CHILDHOOD

How much freedom should parents give their children?

At what age should children be allowed to go places without adult supervision?

Should children be allowed to wear whatever they want?

What is the best way to discipline children?

When does discipline become child abuse?

Should parents bribe their children?

Should parents make their children clean their room?

Do we give children too many trophies?

Are adults hurting young children by pushing them to achieve?

How, and by whom, should children be taught appropriate behavior?

Are "dark"movies okay for kids?

When does a Halloween costume cross the line?

Are parents violating their children's privacy when they share photos and videos of them online?

How young is too young for a smartphone?

Should parents limit how much time children spend on tech devices?

Do parents ever cross the line by helping too much with homework?

Should parents track their teenager's location?

Are you conforming to or rebelling against your parents' wishes for you?

Is childhood today too risk-free?

Is modern culture ruining childhood?

How do you define "family"?

Is it harder to grow up today than it was in the past?

Who should decide if a teenager can get a tattoo or piercing?

What advice would you give mothers or fathers in general—or yours in particular—about how to be better parents?

SCHOOL

Do teachers assign too much homework?

Are high school students being worked too hard?

Does your homework help you learn?

What are you really learning at school?

Does class size matter?

What makes a good teacher?

Do we need a better way to teach math?

Does gym help students perform better in all their classes?

Should kindergarten be more about play or literacy?

What are the best ways to learn about history?

What is the right amount of group work in school?

What do you think of grouping students by ability in schools?

How important is arts education?

Should schools be teaching, and evaluating, social-emotional skills like "grit"?

Do schools provide students with enough opportunities to be creative?

Is Shakespeare too hard?

What have you been taught about slavery?

What role should textbooks play in education?

Are you able to be your real self at school?

Should high schools do more to prepare you for careers?

How much does it matter to you which high school you attend?

Would you rather attend a public or a private high school?

Are small schools more effective than large schools?

Would you want to be home-schooled?

Should home-schoolers be allowed to play public school sports?

Does the way your classroom is decorated affect your learning?

Should all children be able to go to preschool?

Should all students get equal space in a yearbook?
Should schools be allowed to censor school newspapers?
Is your school a safe learning space?
Should schools teach mindfulness?
Are straight A's always a good thing?
Does your teacher's identity affect your learning?
What book would you add to the high school curriculum?
Should schools teach you how to be happy?
Do you feel your school and teachers welcome both liberal and conservative points of view?
How important is knowing how to spell in a Spell-Check world?
How should schools deal with mental health?
Are school dress codes a good idea?
What role should the police have in schools?
What are the best teaching methods for getting students to behave well in class?
Should schools be allowed to use corporal punishment?
Is cheating getting worse?
Should schools put tracking devices in students' ID cards?
Should students be barred from taking cellphones to school?
How should schools address bullying and cyberbullying?
How should schools respond to hazing incidents?
Are there books that should be banned from your school library?
Who should be able to see students' records?
Should schools cancel summer vacation?
Do kids need recess?
Should the school day start later?
Is your school day too short?
Should the dropout age be raised?
Should students be allowed to skip senior year of high school?
Class time + substitute = waste?
Should students be punished for not having lunch money?
Should gifted and talented education be eliminated?

GRADING AND TESTING

Should students be able to grade their teachers?

How well do you think standardized tests measure your abilities?

How seriously should we take standardized tests?

Do you spend too much time preparing for standardized tests?

Should schools offer cash bonuses for good test scores?

How important are parent-teacher conferences?

Should students be present at parent-teacher conferences?

How should parents handle a bad report card?

Does your school hand out too many A's?

Should discomfort excuse students from having to complete an assignment?

COLLEGE AND CAREER

Should a college education be free?

Is college overrated?

Is the college admissions process fair?

Should colleges use admissions criteria other than test scores and grades?

Are early decision programs unfair? Should colleges do away with them?

What criteria should be used in awarding scholarships for college?

Should engineers pay less for college than English majors?

Does it matter where you go to college?

Do college rankings really matter?

Should colleges ban fraternities?

Is a sorority a good place for a feminist?

Should colleges offer degrees in sports?

What do you want more from a career: happiness or wealth?

Would you quit if your values did not match your employer's?

Would you rather work from home or in an office?

Is "doing nothing" a good use of your time?

Should everyone go to college?

Should universities work to curtail student drinking?

Would you pursue a career if you knew you weren't likely to make much money?

Has the cost of college gotten out of hand?

Should colleges contact the families of students who are struggling?

What makes someone a great leader?

How important is related experience in doing a job?

Is it okay to use family connections to get a job?

Are lavish amenities on college campuses useful or frivolous?

How should the problem of sexual assault on college campuses be handled?

Should everyone learn at least one other language?

What are your thoughts on work and "hustle culture"?

Should the work and school week be four days instead of five?

Should stay-at-home parents be paid?

Would you consider serving in the U.S. armed forces?

HEALTH

Should the drinking age be lowered?

Should e-cigarettes be banned for teenagers?

Are antismoking ads effective?

Should marijuana be legal?

Should students be required to take drug tests?

Why is binge drinking so common among young people in the United States?

Should all children be vaccinated?

Should middle school students be drug-tested?

How should schools handle unvaccinated students?

Should physician-assisted suicide be legal in every state?

Do you think a healthier school lunch program is a lost cause?

How concerned are you about where your food comes from?

Is it ethical to eat meat?

What food rules should we try to live by?

Is breakfast really the most important meal of the day?

Do you prefer your tacos "authentic" or "appropriated"?

Should the government tax sugary drinks or limit their size?

Should teenagers think twice before downing energy drinks?

How important is it to be attractive in our society?

What are your opinions on cosmetic surgery?

Do photoshopped images make you feel bad about your own looks?

Would you want to live a life without ever feeling pain?

Would you want to live to 100?

What rules do you have for staying healthy?

Do we worry too much about germs?

Should students get mental health days off from school?

SCIENCE AND THE ENVIRONMENT

How concerned are you about climate change?

How should nations and individuals address climate change?

Should schools teach about climate change?

Should developers be allowed to build in and near the Grand Canyon?

Should scientists try to help people beat old age so we can live longer lives?

Would you change your eating habits to reduce your carbon footprint?

Given unlimited resources, what scientific or medical problem would you investigate?

When is it okay to replace human limbs with technology?

Should fertilized eggs be given legal "personhood"?

Do you think life exists—or has ever existed—somewhere besides Earth?

Will humans live on Mars someday?

Would you want to be a space tourist?

Should we treat robots like people?

Is it ethical to create genetically edited humans?

What were the most important scientific developments this year?

Could you live "plastic free"?

Do you suffer from "nature deficit disorder"?

Would you like to be cryogenically preserved upon your death?

Do we crank up the AC too high?

Should we feel guilty when we travel?

ANIMALS

Should farm animals have more legal protections?

Is it ethical to genetically engineer animals?

Is animal testing ever justified?

Should certain animals have some of the same legal rights as people?

What have you learned from animals?

Is it wrong to focus on animal welfare when humans are suffering?

Do gorillas belong in zoos?

Is it unethical for a zoo to kill a healthy giraffe?

Should circuses be animal-free?

Should you go to jail for kicking a cat?

Should you feel guilty about killing spiders, ants, or other bugs?

Should emotional-support animals be allowed on college campuses?

Are emotional-support animals becoming a scam?

Should we be concerned about where we get our pets?

Should extinct animals be resurrected? If so, which ones?

ETHICS, CHARACTER, AND SPIRITUALITY

Can money buy you happiness?

Which is more important: talent or hard work?

What effect do you think success has on your personal happiness?

How important is keeping your cool?

When should you compromise?

Are we losing the art of listening?

Do people complain too much?

Is "be yourself" bad advice?

Does trying too hard to be happy make us sad?

How important is keeping a clean house, room, or desk?

Do you believe that everything happens for a reason?

How much control do you think you have over your fate?

Does suffering make us stronger and lead to success?

Do bystanders have a responsibility to intervene when there is trouble?

Is looting ever morally okay?

Can you be good without God?

How important do you think it is to marry someone with the same religion?

Are we losing the art of listening?

How much information is "too much information"?

What makes a great conversation?

What role should spirituality play in our lives?

Can kindness become cool?

What is a hero?

Are manners important?

Have curse words become so common they have lost their shock value?

Is one billion too much money for any one person to have?

Should reporters ever help the people they cover?

Should the private lives of famous people be off limits?

Should we make New Year's resolutions?

Would you let a homeless person live in your backyard?

Is struggle essential to happiness?

Should people give money to panhandlers?

What causes should philanthropic groups finance?

Is now the best time in human history to be alive?

Whom do you think has been overlooked by history?

Why should we care about events in other parts of the world?

Is your online world just a "filter bubble" of people with the same opinions?

Why do bystanders sometimes fail to help when they see someone in danger?

Would you return a lost wallet? (What if it had lots of money in it?)

Have you ever quit something? When is that the right or healthy thing to do?

CIVICS, ECONOMICS, AND POLITICS

How strong is your faith in American democracy?

Is America headed in the right direction?

How would *you* describe the state of our union?

Is it possible to start out poor in this country, work hard, and become well-off?

Should the United States care that it's not no. 1?

How should opponents receive a new president—with an open mind and honor for the office, or with defiance and rejection?

What do you think the role of the first lady—or first spouse—should be today?

Should voting be mandatory?

Does voting for a third-party candidate mean throwing away your vote?

If you were governor of your state, how would you spend a budget surplus?

What local problems do you think your mayor should try to solve?

Should rich people have to pay more taxes?

Do you see great disparities of wealth in your community?

What causes should philanthropic groups fund?

What would you do if you were president?

What is more important: our privacy or our national security?

When is the use of military force justified?

When should countries negotiate with their traditional enemies?

Should the United States be spying on its friends?

What responsibility do we have to take in refugees from global humanitarian crises?

Should countries pay ransoms to free hostages held by terrorists?

Should millions of undocumented immigrants be allowed to live in the United States without fear of getting deported?

Are children of undocumented immigrants entitled to a public education?

Do we need a higher minimum wage?

What do we owe our veterans?

Do leaders have moral obligations?

Do great leaders have to be outgoing?

Should the United States get rid of the electoral college?

Should the United States abolish daylight saving time?

Is the American Dream real?

Should celebrities weigh in on politics?

Should Columbus Day be replaced with Indigenous Peoples Day?

Should ex-felons have the right to vote?

When, if ever, should free speech be limited?

Should all Americans receive anti-bias education?

Are we bad citizens if we don't keep up with the news?

Does every country need a "loneliness minister"?

What do you think of President Trump's use of Twitter?

Should national monuments be protected by the government?

Are political memes dangerous to democracy?

Should the government allow "Dreamers" to stay in the United States?

Should Confederate statues be removed or remain in place?

Does the U.S. Constitution need an equal rights amendment?

Do you think you can tell when something is "fake news"?

Do laws that ban offensive words make the world a better place?

Is it important for people with different political beliefs to talk to each other?

Should public transit be free?

GUNS

What are some answers to America's gun violence?

How should we prevent future mass shootings?

Are we becoming numb to school shootings?

Would you feel safer with armed guards patrolling your school?

What is your relationship with guns?

Should teachers be armed with guns?

Where do you stand on unconcealed handguns?

Should guns be permitted on college campuses?

Would arming college students help prevent sexual assaults on campus?

Should the United States ban military-style semiautomatic weapons?

THE JUSTICE SYSTEM

What should be the purpose of prison?

Should prisoners be given the opportunity to get an education?

Should felons be allowed to vote after they have served their time?

Should we abolish the death penalty?

What do you think of the police tactic of stop-and-frisk?

When, if ever, should juvenile offenders receive life sentences?

Do rich people get off easier when they break the law?

Should all police officers wear body cameras?

Should prostitution be legal?

Should texting while driving be treated like drunk driving?

CONSUMER CULTURE

Should we think twice before buying online?

Is Amazon becoming too powerful?

How much do you trust online reviews?

Do you shop at locally owned businesses?

Should companies collect information about you?

Do companies have a responsibility to contribute positively to society?

Should restaurants do away with tipping?

Should single-use plastic shopping bags be banned?

Should politics influence how and where we shop?

Should you care about the health and safety of those making your clothing?

Do you wear clothes for the logo?

Does what you wear say anything about you as a person?

To what company would you write a letter of complaint or admiration?

To what business would you like to give advice?

Could you stop shopping for an entire year?

Is there a "right way" to be a tourist?

Are you an ethical consumer?

Resources

APPENDIX A
Topic Generator

Directions: *Answer the following questions by brainstorming as many fresh responses to each as you can, even if some questions may seem to overlap. The goal is simply to get down as many ideas—large and small—as possible.*

1. What do you care about?
2. What makes you mad?
3. What are you an expert at, no matter how small?
4. What do you like to do in your free time?
5. What do you get that other people don't seem to get? What do you wish more people understood?
6. What do you struggle with?
7. What experiences have you had in your life that have taught you a lot?
8. What do you tend to argue about, whether with your parents, your friends, at school, or online?
9. What communities are you a member of? What issues are important to those communities?
10. What issues in the news have gotten your attention lately?
11. What do you wonder about? What would you like to learn more about?
12. How would you describe yourself? What aspects of your identity are most important to you?
13. What about your own generation, or adults' reactions to it, concerns you?

14. What would you like to see change—about your life, your school, your neighborhood, city or country, our society, or the world?
15. Now look back at what you wrote. What patterns do you see? Do certain topics come up over and over? Which of the things you listed are you most interested in thinking more about right now? Why?
16. Finally, choose one of the things you listed and ask yourself, what issues are there in this topic? What are the questions, controversies, or ongoing discussions in this field that interest you? Then, make a list.

APPENDIX B
Before and After: A Study in Two Essays

Directions: *Both of these drafts are by Nora Fellas, a 2019 winner. With the help of her teacher and some of her classmates, she revised the original to make it fit the 450-word maximum length for our Student Editorial Contest. As you read, you might think about these questions:*

- Which version do you think is stronger? Why?
- What specific changes can you spot?
- Which changes are most notable? Why do you think she made them?
- What can you take away from Nora's process here that might help you with your own?

Early Draft: 743 words

Lessons for 2020 Democratic Presidential Candidates, From a Soon-to-be First-Time Voter

I am one of the more than 5 million people (CENSUS DATA) who is not old enough to vote today, but who will be old enough to vote in the 2020 presidental election. I am writing as a sixteen year old to offer some free lessons to the candidates on how they can earn our votes.

Given the slim margin in the 2016 presidential election, our votes could make all of the difference.

While we have diverse views, the Democrats are likely to have an advantage with young votes given their focus on issues that matter to a large number of us, such as gun control, climate change and women's reproductive rights. In fact, 58 percent of 18–30 year olds identify as Democrats. But this advantage does not guarantee success against the presumptive Republican nominee, Donald Trump.

But, since, historically, the turnout rate for young voters is low, what can the candidates do to inspire us to show up?

First, be authentic. While I supported Hillary Clinton over Trump in the last election, her attempts to reach young voters ran felt phony and condescending. I recall a particularly cringey video in which Hillary said, "Pokemon Go to the polls," referring to an app popular among middle and high school kids, Pokemon Go. We see it again this time around with Elizabeth Warren's attempt to appear relatable by drinking a beer Instagram livestream. While social media is the right medium to reach the young voter—as both AOC and Beto O'Rourke can attest. One Boston Herald analyst criticized the image of the, "multi-million-dollar Cambridge law professor poppin' a brewski on New Year's Eve." She didn't start the video already drinking a beer, she announced to the camera, "I'm gonna get me a beer," because she wanted to present an image of a relatable candidate. She also had her husband as a prop and expressed surprise to see him in their own house. It's not believable to young people that Elizabeth Warren casually opened up Instagram and decided to do a livestream without advising from her team. It feels contrived and the opposite of what she is trying to project: that she's down to earth.

In the 2016 election, Hillary and Trump both tried to appeal to young people. Trump did this through Twitter, which is mostly used by 30 year olds and younger. He ran a campaign based in unapologetic truth, a rejection of political correctness. Hillary, in response, ran a campaign that felt phony and condescending. I recall a particularly cringey video in which Hillary said, "Pokemon Go to the polls." She was referencing the app of the summer, Pokemon Go, which was mostly trendy among middle and high school aged kids. First, this was a mistake because it was clear that she had been fed that line and had no idea what she was talking about. Second, it felt condescending, as if youth votes could be bought by name dropping an ios game.

Of course, there needs to be an appeal to youth voters, but candidates must be wary of seeming out of touch. The youth vote is not to be taken for granted. In fact, in the 2016 election, while 70 percent of citizens 65 years and older voted, and around 60 percent of 44–64 year olds did, only about 46 percent of 18–29 year olds voted. (CENSUS) The key difference between my generation and my parents' generation, is that I am part of the "Bernie or Bust" generation. As we saw in 2016, young people will not choose between what they feel is "the lesser of two evils," they will simply stay home if neither candidate inspires them.

That is why politicians need to take their appeal to the youth seriously, and stop with the pandering. Take Sanders, for example, he is nearly eighty years old, he could not be more different from the youth voters. He doesn't use Instagram, because it wouldn't come off as authentic, and he is incredibly popular among the youth—because he supports free college and DACA.

To the 2020 candidates: The key to earning my vote, and the votes of my peers is not showing us how "cool" you are by using slang. We don't want to see that you can take the advice of your millennial intern, we want to see that your original ideas reflect the issues that affect us, like gun control and climate change—otherwise, we will just stay home.

Final Draft: 450 words

Lessons for 2020 Democratic Presidential Candidates, From a Soon-to-be First-Time Voter, by Nora Fellas, 16

I am one of more than five million people too young to vote today, but who will be old enough in 2020. I am 16, I run a political blog with over 100,000 followers, and I am offering some free lessons to candidates on how they can earn our votes.

Given the slim margin in the 2016 election, our votes could make all the difference. So listen up.

While young people have diverse views, Democrats focus on issues that matter to many of us, like gun control and climate change, making them more attractive than the presumptive Republican nominee,

President Trump. The challenge for Democratic candidates is to distinguish themselves to capture the youth vote.

So what actually matters to us? It's simple, but elusive: authenticity.

When politicians force relatability, they seem fake. Prior to her bid, Elizabeth Warren Instagram livestreamed and began by announcing to the camera, "I'm gonna get me a beer," and then thanked her husband for being there, in their own house, as if it hadn't all been scripted. One *Boston Herald* analyst criticized the image of the "multi-million-dollar Cambridge law professor poppin' a brewski." It's not credible that Warren opened Instagram and decided to livestream of her own volition.

In 2016, Secretary Clinton and Trump both tried to appeal to young people. Trump used Twitter, and his statements were so unfiltered that they could only have come from him. Clinton's messaging, however, felt phony. In a particularly cringey video, Clinton said, "Pokemon Go to the polls," referencing the tween-trending app of that summer, Pokemon Go. It was clear that she had been fed that line and it felt condescending, suggesting youth votes could be earned by name-dropping a game.

This isn't to say candidates shouldn't appeal to young people—they must, because our votes can't be taken for granted. In 2016, 18–29 year olds had the lowest turnout of any age group. The key difference between our generation and our parents' is that we belong to the "Bernie or Bust" generation. 2016 revealed that we won't choose between "the lesser of two evils"; if no candidate inspires us, we will just stay home.

This is why politicians need to appeal seriously to youth voters. Take Sanders: he is nearly 80, yet he is incredibly popular among young people. Why? Not because of his Instagram skills, but because he's perceived as genuine—his politics haven't changed.

To the 2020 candidates: the key to earning our vote isn't pandering to us. Rather, we want to see that you genuinely care about the issues that matter to us. If you do that, you won't need to worry about spreading your message on Instagram. We'll do it for you.

APPENDIX C
A Sample Essay Annotated with the Comments of Our Judges

Quotes in the annotations were taken from an actual discussion among seven staff members.

"Nothing Gets Between Me and My Sushi . . . Except Plastic, Maybe"

Learning Network Staff Member: "Already I'm interested because of this unique, voicey headline."

As an Asian-American self-proclaimed millennial foodie, imagine the shock I experienced when I discovered a horrifying truth—plastic cuisine. Ubiquitous plastic extends beyond our surroundings—and invades our guts—through what we eat and drink. I first learned that sushi is chock-full of microplastics. There's so much plastic in the water, churned down to the size of rice grains or smaller, and fish gobble it up. When the fish end up on our dinner plates, guess what? Our bellies receive an unsettling supplement that wasn't on the menu.

"From the beginning I have a sense of a real person in this essay, of who's talking and why this topic matters to them."

"The standout thing about this essay is the voice. Look at all these different playful words—'bellies,' 'gobble,' 'yonder,' 'gross.'" Even 'tummy,' which could have been too much, but this person gets away with it. He or she seems like a real kid, but a kid who is using language strategically."

In fact, a National Geographic study found microplastics in 114 marine species—with over half of them regulars in restaurants—meaning that my tummy acquires some uninvited non-digestible additives.

"Yet this is also a kid who can command scientific evidence in a sophisticated way to back up what they're is saying. This sentence is a good example of the playful/serious mix in this whole essay."

Even water isn't safe! My parents often tell me to drink more water to wash down my food—but did they know that I was ingesting plastic too? A 2017 study by Orb Media found microplastic contamination in 83 percent of global tap water—with the highest amount, 94 percent, found in the United States!

You may wonder: So what? Has there been a study that proves housing microplastics inside of your body is harmful? Not yet, but still. Firstly—it's gross! I'm eating a material that's meant to last beyond a thousand years, and will probably accompany my skeleton long after I putrefy in my grave.

Imagine the surplus of chemicals needed to make these durable particles. National Geographic highlighted a few chemicals contained in plastic with the potential to become poisons in certain doses: "endocrine disruptors—chemicals that interfere with normal hormone function, even contribute to weight gain. Flame retardants may interfere with brain development in fetuses and children; other compounds that cling to plastics can cause cancer or birth defects."

By informing you of this ongoing crisis, am I telling you to give up seafood? Never!

Personally, and I think I can speak for many fellow foodies, nothing gets in between me and my sushi. Instead, let's stop dismissing the old-school motto: reuse, reduce, and recycle. Seriously—no more Acme bags that drift yonder with the wind, and take a hint from good ol' Trader Joes for the more environmentally friendly alternatives. Sure, paper bags may be more fragile, and fabric ones are often more expensive, but that's a small price to pay for potentially saving a sea creature that would have been strangled or starved otherwise.

"This, for me, was one too many exclamation points. This student is walking a fine line with voice here, and though this might seem small, the use of an exclamation point here undermines the seriousness of what he or she is trying to say."

"In this paragraph the writer takes risky chances with voice, language, and tone. For me, it works, but I could see 'Not yet, but still. Firstly—it's gross!' turning some readers off. Plus, is this the counterclaim?—I would have liked more depth and detail here—what IS known about this issue?"

"This paragraph does a good job of bolstering the argument with real detail, even if this person doesn't go quite far enough in making the case that these chemicals are reaching us in dangerous levels."

"Well done call-back to the title, and the 'call to action' is personal and doable. So many students stumble by taking on too much—'The earth is in trouble! We must do something now!'—but this writer makes it small, personal, actionable.

"The use of words like "we" "our" and "us"—and, here, "let's"—is deft. It really shows awareness of the reader and engages us in a way that persuades but doesn't hector. Let's solve this together!"

"I started to question this writer's whole essay a bit at this point. There's a lot of leaps that aren't justified well enough. Is individual use of plastic really the culprit, or is it more from industry? The causes and effects of plastics in the water aren't fully addressed."

Let's cut down on the plastic, and the next time you're tempted to innocuously trash some plastic straws, just remember that same "harmless" plastic is somewhere puncturing a turtle's brain through its nostril and killing a fish through literally explosive bowels . . . and its next stop?

"The language here and in the piece overall really provokes. I reacted more to this essay, to be honest, than I have to any kind of opinion piece I've read in a long time—by a kid OR by an adult."

Your stomach.

"A very bold ending, but it works—and loops back to the title and the beginning. Overall, after reading hundreds of essays that kind of merge together in my mind this piece was a real bright spot ... In the end, it does what it's supposed to do: it convinces us to take our use of plastic more seriously."

Sources

Kosuth, Mary, et al. "Synthetic Polymer Contamination In Global Drinking Water." Orb Media, 16 May 2017.

Quenqua, Douglas. "Microplastics Find Their Way Into Your Gut, a Pilot Study Finds." The New York Times, 22 Oct. 2018.

Royte, Elizabeth. "We Know Plastic Is Harming Marine Life. What About Us?" National Geographic, June 2018.

Wassener, Bettina. "Fish Ingesting Plastic Waste, Study Finds." The New York Times, 8 July 2011.

APPENDIX D

The Rubric and Rules for the NYTLN Student Editorial Contest

RUBRIC AND RULES FOR THE NEW YORK TIMES LEARNING NETWORK ANNUAL STUDENT EDITORIAL CONTEST

Rules:

1. You can write your editorial about any topic you like, as long as you use at least one source from The Times.
2. Use at least one non-Times source. But make sure that the source you use is a reliable one. We encourage you to find sources that offer different perspectives on an issue.
3. Always cite your sources. Our submission form contains a required field for entering your citations. We include an example as well, though you can use M.L.A. or A.P.A. styles, or just list the web addresses. Even if you use a print source or an expert interview, you must provide a citation. Readers (and judges) should always be able to tell where you got your evidence. However, there is no need to provide in-text citations.
4. The editorial must not exceed 450 words. Your title and list of sources are separate, however, and do not count as part of your 450-word limit.
5. Have an opinion. Editorials are different from news articles because they try to persuade readers to share your point of view. Don't be afraid to take a stand.
6. Write your editorial by yourself or with a group, but please submit

only one editorial per student. If you are working as a team, just remember to submit all of your names when you post your entry. And if you're submitting as part of a team, you should not also submit as an individual.

7. Be original and use appropriate language. Write for a well-informed audience, but include enough background information to give context. Be careful not to plagiarize. Use quotation marks around lines you take verbatim from another source, or rephrase and cite your source.
8. We will use the rubric below to judge entries, and the winning editorials will be featured on The Learning Network. Your work will be judged by Times journalists, Learning Network staff members and educators from around the country.

THE NEW YORK TIMES LEARNING NETWORK STUDENT EDITORIAL CONTEST RUBRIC

	Excellent (4)	Proficient (3)	Developing (2)	Beginning (1)
Viewpoint: Editorial states a clear opinion and issues a call to action through argument based on evidence.				
Evidence: Editorial uses compelling evidence to support the opinion, and cites reliable sources.				
Analysis and Persuasion: Editorial convincingly argues point of view by providing relevant background information, using valid examples, acknowledging counter-claims, and developing claims—all in a clear and organized fashion.				
Language: Editorial has a strong voice and engages the reader. It uses language, style and tone appropriate to its purpose and features correct grammar, spelling and punctuation.				
Guidelines: Editorial follows all contest guidelines, including the citation of at least one Times and one non-Times source				

APPENDIX E

Essays for Teaching Various Elements of Argument

The essays listed below were chosen for this chart because they are among the clearest examples in each category to share with students. To find many more examples, and to read in detail about how to use all of them as models, please see the corresponding sections of this Teacher's Companion.

If you would like to show your students . . .	Here are some clear examples from the anthology:
Essays that are less traditional and break what students may consider to be the "rules" of argument writing	Start with essays 47 and 62
Essays that are more traditional and generally follow those rules	Essays 16, 37, 42, 78, and 89
Essays that use the appeal of personal authority and experience (*ethos*)	Essays 19, 45, 57, 68, and 92
Essays that have strong appeals to fact and reason (*logos*)	Essays 29, 64, 82, 90, and 96
Essays that tell stories and appeal to emotion (*pathos*)	Essays 3, 46, 53, 70, and 85
Essays that show how to connect personal experience to a larger point	Essays 4, 9, 31, 87, and 99

Essays that "start with a bang"	Essays 10, 32, 36, 39, and 48
Essays that engage counterarguments well	Essays 12, 20, 55, 59, and 71
Essays that issue strong calls to action	Essays 27, 35, 49, 74, and 77
Essays that play with voice, language, and tone	Essays 8, 13, 30, 51, and 76
Essays with memorable conclusions	Essays 5, 17, 23, 33, and 40

References

1. Grant Wiggins, "Real-World Writing: Making Purpose and Audience Matter," *English Journal 98*, no. 5 (2009).
2. Unit 5: Argumentative Writing, The New York Times Learning Network, Feb. 5, 2020. https://www.nytimes.com/2020/02/12/learning/unit-5-argumentative-writing.html
3. Beth Pandolpho, "Reader Idea: Helping Students Discover and Write About the Issues That Matter to Them," The New York Times Learning Network, Feb. 20, 2019. https://www.nytimes.com/2019/02/20/learning/reader-idea-helping-students-discover-and-write-about-the-issues-that-matter-to-them.html
4. Sam Leith, "Other Men's Flowers," *The New York Times*, Sept. 8, 2012. https://opinionator.blogs.nytimes.com/2012/09/08/other-mens-flowers/
5. Fry, Richard and Kim Parker, "Early Benchmarks Show 'Post-Millennials' on Track to Be Most Diverse, Best-Educated Generation Yet." Pew Research Center, Nov. 15, 2018. https://www.pewsocialtrends.org/2018/11/15/early-benchmarks-show-post-millennials-on-track-to-be-most-diverse-best-educated-generation-yet/
6. Kim Parker, Nikki Graf, and Ruth Igielnik, "Generation Z Looks a Lot Like Millennials on Key Social and Political Issues," Pew Research Center, Jan. 17, 2019. https://www.pewsocialtrends.org/2019/01/17/generation-z-looks-a-lot-like-millennials-on-key-social-and-political-issues/
7. Rudine Sims Bishop, "Mirrors, Windows and Sliding Glass Doors," *Perspectives: Choosing and Using Books for the Classroom*, vol. 6, no. 3 (1990).
8. Katherine Schulten, "Making Connections: 53 Teenagers Suggest Creative Ways to Link School Curriculum to the World of 2019," The New York Times Learning Network, March 7, 2019. https://www.nytimes

.com/2019/03/07/learning/making-connections-53-teenagers-suggest-creative-ways-to-link-school-curriculum-to-the-world-of-2019.html

9. Webinar, "Teaching Argument Writing With Nicholas Kristof and The New York Times," YouTube https://www.youtube.com/watch?v=Z_miFxULbAc
10. Sondra Perl, *Felt Sense: Writing with the Body.* (Portsmouth, NH: Heinemann, 2004).
11. Trish Hall, *Writing to Persuade* (New York: Liveright, 2019).
12. Hall.
13. Wiggins, Grant, "Real-World Writing: Making Purpose and Audience Matter," Eng*lish Journal 98*, No. 5 (2009)
14. Jennifer Fletcher, *Teaching Arguments* (Portland, ME: Stenhouse Publishers, 2015).
15. Jacqueline Hesse and Christine McCartney, "Reader Idea: A New Research and Argument-Writing Approach Helps Students Break Out of the Echo Chamber," The New York Times Learning Network, Feb. 20, 2019. https://www.nytimes.com/2019/02/19/learning/reader-idea-a-new-research-and-argument-writing-approach-helps-students-break-out-of-the-echo-chamber.html
16. Ahmed, Sara K., *Being the Change: Lessons and Strategies to Teach Social Comprehension*, Portsmouth, N.H., 2018.
17. Katherine Schulten, "Improving Your News Diet: A Three-Step Lesson Plan for Teenagers and Teachers," The New York Times Learning Network, Nov. 2, 2017. https://www.nytimes.com/2017/11/02/learning/lesson-plans/improving-your-news-diet-a-three-step-lesson-plan-for-teenagers-and-teachers.html
18. Katherine Schulten, "10 Things We Learned About Teenagers and the News: The Results of Our Student 'News Diet' Challenge," The New York Times Learning Network, Feb. 1, 2018. https://www.nytimes.com/2018/02/01/learning/10-things-we-learned-about-teenagers-and-the-news-the-results-of-our-student-news-diet-challenge.html
19. Kenneth Burke, *The Philosophy of Literary Form: Studies in Symbolic Action* (Oakland, CA: University of California press, 1973).
20. Room for Debate, *The New York Times*, https://www.nytimes.com/roomfordebate

21. "Should Every Young Athlete Get a Trophy?" *The New York Times*, Oct. 6, 2016.https://www.nytimes.com/roomfordebate/2016/10/06/should-every-young-athlete-get-a-trophy
22. Hesse and McCartney.
23. "Middle Ground" series, Jubilee Media, YouTube, https://www.youtube.com/playlist?list=PLBVNJo7nhINRNiv8B_GuRP_gWEFRwrdTT
24. Donald M. Murray, "Making Meaning Clear: The Logic of Revision," *Journal of Basic Writing* 03.3 (1981).
25. Pandolpho.
26. Linda Friedrich, "Engaging Youth in Civic Action Through Writing," The Teaching Channel, March 7, 2018. https://learn.teachingchannel.com/blog/2018/03/07/civic-action-through-writing/
27. Jay Heinrichs, *Thank You for Arguing: What Aristotle, Lincoln, and Homer Simpson Can Teach Us About the Art of Persuasion* (New York: Three Rivers Press, 2007).
28. Kristof, Nicholas, "This Is What a Refugee Looks Like," The New York Times, Feb. 3, 2017.
29. Jason Spingarn-Koff, "How to Write an Editorial," The New York Times Learning Network, Feb.5, 2014. https://learning.blogs.nytimes.com/2014/02/06/student-contest-write-an-editorial-on-an-issue-that-matters-to-you/
30. Fletcher.
31. Amanda Christy Brown, "I Don't Think So: Writing Effective Counterarguments," The New York Times Learning Network, Feb. 2, 2015. https://learning.blogs.nytimes.com/2015/02/12/i-dont-think-so-writing-effective-counterarguments/
32. "Somewhere Between," directed by Linda Goldstein Knowlton (Ladylike Films: 2011).
33. Noden, Harry, *Image Grammar,* Portsmouth, N.H.: Heinemann Publishers, 1999.
34. Spingarn-Koff.
35. Schulten, "Writing for an Audience Beyond the Teacher." https://www.nytimes.com/2018/11/15/learning/writing-for-audience-beyond-teacher.html

36. Meredith Colias-Pete, "Gary teens picked for New York Times podcast contest have 'the willingness to be bold and ask questions'." *The Chicago Post-Tribune,* Nov. 16, 2018. https://www.chicagotribune.com/suburbs/post-tribune/ct-ptb-gary-steel-city-podcast-st-20181109-story.html
37. Proulx, Natalie, "Should Schools Teach You How to be Happy?" New York Times Learning Network, Feb. 1, 2018. https://www.nytimes.com/2018/02/01/learning/should-schools-teach-you-how-to-be-happy.html
38. Schulten, "Writing for an Audience Beyond the Teacher."

About the Author

Katherine Schulten was editor-in-chief of The New York Times Learning Network from 2006 to 2019 and is still a contributing editor there. She grew up in Texas and began her career in education right after college, when she served as a Jesuit Volunteer with middle school students in Brooklyn, New York. From there, she briefly taught in Japan, then spent 10 years as an English teacher at Brooklyn's Edward R. Murrow High School, where she was also advisor to the school newspaper.

After winning a Prudential Fellowship to the Columbia School of Journalism, Katherine worked for nine years in schools all over the city as a literacy consultant for the New York City Writing Project. In that role she focused on Career and Technical Education, helping teachers infuse writing into subjects across the curriculum, from science and math to plumbing and cosmetology.

Katherine is also on the board of Literacy for Incarcerated Teens, a non profit which gets books and writing programs into New York state detention facilities for young people. She lives in Brooklyn with her husband and is the mother of twins now in their twenties.